DEAR JEFF AND SHAUNTI,

MW01232753

ng
cRipT
EMENT.

John

Answer the Prayer of Jesus

The House of Prisca and Aquila

Our mission at the House of Prisca and Aquila is to produce quality books that expound accurately the word of God to empower women and men to minister together in a multicultural church. Our writers have a positive view of the Bible as God's revelation that affects both thoughts and words, so it is plenary, historically accurate, and consistent in itself, fully reliable, and authoritative as God's revelation. Because God is true, God's revelation is true, inclusive to men and women and speaking to a multicultural church, wherein all the diversity of the church is represented within the parameters of egalitarianism and inerrancy.

The word of God is what we are expounding, thereby empowering women and men to minister together in all levels of the church and home. The reason we say women and men together is because that is the model of Prisca and Aquila, ministering together to another member of the church—Apollos: "Having heard Apollos, Priscilla and Aquila took him aside and more accurately expounded to him the Way of God" (Acts 18:26). True exposition, like true religion, is by no means boring—it is fascinating. Books that reveal and expound God's true nature "burn within us" as they elucidate the Scripture and apply it to our lives.

This was the experience of the disciples who heard Jesus on the road to Emmaus: "Were not our hearts burning while Jesus was talking to us on the road, while he was opening the scriptures to us?" (Luke 24:32). We are hoping to create the classics of tomorrow, significant and accessible trade and academic books that "burn within us."

Our "house" is like the home to which Prisca and Aquila no doubt brought Apollos as they took him aside. It is like the home in Emmaus where Jesus stopped to break bread and reveal his presence. It is like the house built on the rock of obedience to Jesus (Matt 7:24). Our "house," as a euphemism for our publishing team, is a home where truth is shared and Jesus' Spirit breaks bread with us, nourishing all of us with his bounty of truth.

We are delighted to work together with Wipf and Stock in this series and welcome submissions on a wide variety of topics from an egalitarian inerrantist global perspective. The House of Prisca and Aquila is also a ministry center affiliated with the International Council of Community Churches.

For more information, contact housepriscaaquila@comcast.net.

Answer the Prayer of Jesus

A Call for Biblical Unity

JOHN P. LATHROP

WIPF & STOCK · Eugene, Oregon

ANSWER THE PRAYER OF JESUS
A Call for Biblical Unity

House of Prisca and Aquila Series

Wipf & Stock
An Imprint of Wipf and Stock Publishers
199 W. 8th Ave., Suite 3
Eugene, OR 97401

www.wipfandstock.com

ISBN 13: 978-1-60899-392-5

Manufactured in the U.S.A.

This book is dedicated to the accomplishment
of the greater purposes of God.

Contents

Preface

BEFORE READING THIS BOOK it might be helpful for you to understand something of my spiritual history. I was born and raised in a Roman Catholic family. We were the practicing kind, attending church each week, observing the Holy Days, and partaking of the sacraments in keeping with the teachings of the church. In addition to attending church, I became active in the service of the church at a young age. I served as an altar boy from the time I was in the fourth grade right up into my freshman year in college. After I stopped serving as an altar boy, I began playing guitar at the Folk Mass that was held at my home church. The music at the Folk Mass was less traditional than what one would typically hear at a Catholic service. The service used guitars, instead of an organ, for musical accompaniment. This slightly more contemporary service enjoyed some popularity in the Roman Catholic Church in the 1970s.

In my early twenties I went on a bit of a spiritual excursion which took me to the Charismatic Movement in the Catholic Church, to the Episcopal Church, and to the Mormon Church. A few times in the midst of this spiritual journey I prayed "the sinner's prayer." I believe that my salvation "really took" when I was twenty-five years old. At that time I gave my heart to the Lord through the ministry of an Advent Christian pastor. My wife and I then began to attend the Advent Christian church regularly; we were both baptized in that church. When we first began attending the church, it was very charismatic, much like a Pentecostal church.

Shortly after I came to the Lord, I had a desire to go into ministry. I applied to Berkshire Christian College, an Advent Christian college that was located in Lenox, Massachusetts. I eventually visited the school and had an interview with the dean. I did not wind up going to Bible school at that time because of concerns I had about how I would be able to go to school and work in order to provide for my wife and our daughter.

A few years later my wife and I moved our membership to the local Assemblies of God church. While we were there I once again had a desire to go into the ministry. This time I did follow through, and in 1981 my wife and I and now our three children moved to Rhode Island where I became a student at Zion Bible Institute (now Zion Bible College). At that time Zion was an independent Pentecostal school.

After I graduated from Zion I applied for, and received, ministerial credentials with the Christian Church of North America (CCNA). The Christian Church of North America was a classical Pentecostal denomination with an Italian ethnic heritage. The denomination has recently changed its name and is now known as the International Fellowship of Christian Assemblies. I still hold credentials with this fellowship today.

In 1997 I decided to go back to school to get a Master's Degree. I applied to and was accepted at a non-denominational school, Gordon-Conwell Theological Seminary. Specifically, I attended Gordon-Conwell's Center for Urban Ministerial Education (CUME). This proved to be a very rich and positive experience for me as I was educated with, and by, people who were ethnically and denominationally different than me. As you can see, in the course of my spiritual journey I have spent time in both the Catholic and Protestant branches of the church and have been exposed to both liturgical and freestyle church services. I have, in some small way, experienced the diversity that can be found in the body of Christ.

Acknowledgements

I COULD NOT HAVE written this book alone; I have been helped along the way by many people. I would like to start by thanking the House of Prisca and Aquila staff, especially Drs. William and Aída Spencer, for believing in this book. They accepted the proposal for the book and were enthusiastic about it from the beginning. Thanks to the staff at Wipf and Stock who guided the manuscript through the various stages of production to its final form. I also wish to thank my wife, Cynthia. She gave me the idea to expand the vision of this book and make it more global in perspective. She also allowed me to put many hours into writing undisturbed. Thanks also go to Dr. Royce Gruenler, New Testament professor emeritus at Gordon-Conwell Theological Seminary, for reading the manuscript and offering helpful suggestions for improvement. I thankfully acknowledge the technical expertise of Esmé Bieberly who served as my copy editor. I am grateful to David Manuel for granting me permission to quote freely from his book, *Like a Mighty River*. I am also grateful to the Lorenz Corporation for allowing me to use some of the lyrics of the song, "They'll Know We Are Christians." Some of the information in chapter 8 was supplied by Daniel Lawry, Sondra and Mario Chisari, and my son, Daniel Lathrop. I appreciate their help. The global section of the book would not have been possible without the help of my international contacts. The following people helped me in this regard: Rev. Nancy Hudson, Jackie Thomas and Martin De Lange (South Africa), Pastor Sammy Nyranga (Kenya), Irene Nambajjwe, Annette Tusabe, and Jonathan Luutu (Uganda), Dr. Finny Philip (India), and Pastors Ben Chew and

Daniel Chua (Singapore). Thanks to all of you; I couldn't have done it without you. May you be blessed for your service to the Lord and to me.

Introduction

WHEN WE THINK OF Jesus and prayer, our minds probably gravitate in one of two directions. First, we may think about Jesus' prayer life. Jesus was most definitely a man of prayer; he prayed early in the morning (Mark 1:35), all night (Luke 6:12), for others (Luke 22:31–32; 23:34), and for himself (Matt 26:39). Jesus not only practiced prayer, he was passionate about it. The writer to the Hebrews tells us that Jesus prayed with tears and loud cries (Heb 5:7). He was such a model of prayer that one of his disciples asked him to teach them to pray (Luke 11:1).

The second way that we might typically think about Jesus and prayer is with reference to Jesus answering our prayers. Jesus himself said that if we ask anything in his name we will have the request that we make (John 14:13–14). This is why many Christians make their requests in the name of Jesus. We all have many needs, and we want the Lord to intervene on our behalf and meet them.

One thing that we probably almost never think about regarding Jesus and prayer is we ourselves being the answer to a prayer of Jesus. After all, how could we be? Jesus lived in the first century, and we live in the twenty-first century. Besides, he did not make a specific request, did he? Well, he did make a request, but he did not address it to us but to his Father. The request that he made was very dear to his heart. The question is this: will we be the answer to the prayer that Jesus prayed? Will we, knowing what he has prayed, seek to fall in line with his desire? My hope is that as you read this book you will want to be a part of the answer.

In his book *A House United,* Francis Frangipane writes about being an answer to the prayer of Jesus.[1] That is what this book is about. As Pastor Wayne Cordeiro has written, after all of the prayers that Jesus has personally answered on our behalf, wouldn't it be nice for us to answer just one prayer that he prayed?[2] It seems very appropriate. May the Lord help us to understand Jesus' prayer and work toward its fulfillment. Be assured that this will not be an easy task but one that will require some effort on our part once we understand the heart of the Lord. Jesus' prayer in John 17 will be the basis for this book. As we make our way forward, we will note the challenges to the prayer's fulfillment, and cite examples of the challenges being met and the obstacles overcome. This book will have a "grass roots" feel to it. A lot of what you will read has come from my own experience. The material in the international reports, found in chapter 10, has, for the most part, come from a network of personal connections that I have been able to make around the world. As you read this book, please note that many of the steps being taken toward unity are voluntary. That is, the people of God are moving in this direction entirely on their own; they are not being "forced" by organizations. I think this is significant (and a work of the Spirit). Be encouraged that though answering the prayer of Jesus may at times be challenging, it is not "mission impossible." The journey could prove to be very interesting and rewarding, and it will serve to advance the kingdom.

1. Frangipane, *A House United,* 153.
2. Cordeiro, *Doing Church as a Team,* 15.

1

The Prayer of Jesus

IN JOHN 17 WE find the longest recorded prayer of Jesus; the apostle John, under the guidance of the Holy Spirit, included it in his gospel. In fact, it is preserved for us only in John's gospel. Jesus prayed this prayer just prior to his arrest and subsequent crucifixion. The prayer is very significant for a number of reasons: because it is included in the Scriptures; because Jesus, the Son of God, prayed it; and because of its content. As you read through the prayer you will see that Jesus was anticipating a time of transition, a time when he would be leaving the world and his disciples, to rejoin his Father in Heaven (John 17:11, 13). As this time of transition drew near, Jesus offered up this prayer. In his prayer he made a number of requests; he prayed for himself and he also prayed for his disciples. A quick reading of the prayer will show that the majority of his prayer was given over to making requests for his followers. In this chapter we will focus our attention on the portion of the prayer that he offered for his disciples. This section of his prayer falls into two parts; there is a section given to prayer for the disciples who were present with him in the first century, and a section given to prayer for the disciples who were yet to come. Let us briefly consider each of the parts of the prayer that Jesus prayed for his disciples.

JESUS' PRAYER FOR HIS DISCIPLES WHO WERE PRESENT WITH HIM

In the first part of his prayer for his followers Jesus prayed for the disciples who were present with him (John 17:6–19). As he prayed, he acknowledged the good spiritual qualities in his disciples' lives. He said that they knew that everything that Jesus had came from the Father (John 17:7), that they accepted the words that Jesus gave to them, that they knew with certainty that Jesus came from the Father, and that they believed that the Father sent Jesus into the world (John 17:8). In short, his disciples had some spiritual perception; this was because they had received divine revelation. One example of this is the Lord's words to Peter; he told Peter that he was able to make the declaration that Jesus was the Christ because it had been revealed to him by the Father (Matt 16:17). After listing these positive qualities of his followers, which were clear evidence of the work of God in their lives, Jesus moved on to make some requests on their behalf. His requests included prayers for their unity, protection (John 17:11, 15), and sanctification (John 17:17). These requests, at least in part, arose out of Jesus' concern for his followers. He knew that he was no longer going to physically be with them to help them as he had been in the past (John 17:12), so he asked the Father to minister to them and meet their needs. The disciples had already endured harsh treatment in the world (John 17:14), and they would again as the book of Acts makes clear (Acts 4:1–22; 5:17–40; 8:1–3; 12:1–19). In addition to harsh treatment from people, the attacks of the evil one would be directed toward them as well (John 17:15); these things caused Jesus to intercede for his followers. Jesus wanted his followers to be sanctified, or set apart as God's people in the world. But Jesus' prayer for his followers didn't end there; it went on.

JESUS' PRAYER FOR HIS FUTURE DISCIPLES

Beginning at John 17:20, Jesus starts to pray for the people who will come to believe in him though the ministry of the first-century disciples, those who were with him at the time he prayed. This part of the prayer, though not specifically directed toward the first-century disciples, may have been very encouraging to them because it showed that they would have fruit from their ministry: people would come to believe in Jesus through their word (John 17:20) as they ministered in the world (John 17:18). In fact, the fruit that would come from their ministry would be more than they could see, or perhaps even imagine. This prayer applies not only to those who would directly hear their testimony or preaching, such as those who responded to Peter's message on the Day of Pentecost (see Acts 2), but also to all of those who would come to faith in Jesus through their word, the apostolic writings contained in the New Testament.[1] The apostle John specifically says that he wrote his gospel for the purpose of leading people to faith in Jesus (John 20:30–31). So the prayer of Jesus is very comprehensive; it applies to believers from the first century, right on through to the end of church history. This being the case, if you are a Christian, Jesus' prayer in John 17 applies to you! With that said, let us now turn our attention to what Jesus asked for his followers.

In John 17:21, Jesus prayed that his people would be one; a couple of verses later in John 17:23, he asked that they would be united. Different words were used, but the requests are basically the same: Jesus prayed for the unity of his people. Jesus prayed twice for the same thing, and he made these requests in very close proximity to one another. The repetition of the request seems to be important; Jesus appears to be stressing this request, emphasizing it. This prayer reveals some very significant things; let us now take a closer look at this prayer of Jesus.

---

1. Stott, *The Spirit, the Church and the World*, 82.

WHAT THIS PRAYER REVEALS

The Heart of God

One thing that this prayer reveals is the heart of God, that is, God's desire for his people. Jesus and the Father are distinct persons within the Godhead (see Matt 3:16–17; 17:1–8; 28:19), but they are united in purpose (John 5:19). The unity of the Father and Jesus the Son can be seen in a number of biblical texts. Three times in this prayer in John 17 Jesus refers to his unity with the Father; twice he says that he and the Father are one (John 17:11, 22), and once he expresses the same thought without using those exact words (John 17:21). The unity of the Father and the Son can be seen in other texts as well. In John 10:30 Jesus plainly says, "I and the Father are one." Earlier in his gospel John tells us that the one whom God has sent, Jesus, speaks the words of God (John 3:34). During his earthly ministry, Jesus said that to see him was to see the Father (John 14:9). Jesus also said that he only did what he saw the Father doing (John 5:19). Jesus was, and is, always in perfect harmony with the plans, purposes, and works of the Father. Since these things are true, Jesus always prayed in the will of God; he always asked what the Father would want asked. The requests that Jesus made in this prayer in John 17 are God's will for his people. This shows us that God's desire, God's heart, for his people is that they be united.

The Need of Humanity

Jesus' prayer also shows us is that there is a need for the kind of prayer that he prayed. Jesus is not one to waste his time on frivolous, or meaningless, activities. Jesus knew that unity would be a challenge for his people, so he prayed about the matter. In fact, the need was so great that he did not refer it to an intercessory prayer group; he prayed for it himself! It is obviously a very significant need if the Son of God prays for something. Jesus was very much aware of the difficulties or challenges that the disciples would face with regard to the issue of unity. He saw evidence of some of these problems early on in the lives of his followers. The disciples talked about which of them was the greatest, or most important, on a number of occasions (Mark 9:34; Luke 22:24). James and John sought places of honor for themselves in Jesus' kingdom, which resulted in the other disciples becoming upset with them (Mark 10:35–41). Jesus' disciples also were concerned when they saw someone, who was not a part of their group, doing works in Jesus' name (Mark 9:38). These are just a few examples, but they demonstrate that unity was a problem for the followers of Jesus from the very beginning of the Christian movement. Subsequent church history has not fared any better; in fact, it is probably worse. Church history records many instances in which the body of Christ has divided. This confirms that the prayer that Jesus prayed for unity among his people was, and is, a very necessary prayer.

Jesus' Care for His People

A third thing that Jesus' prayer shows us is his care for his people. We typically pray for people that we care about; Jesus does the same. He prays for all of his followers, and note that there is no partiality in his prayer; he makes the same requests for all of his children in all ages. The requests that he makes are for good things. He does not want his people to be destroyed by the enemy (John 17:15), nor does he want them to be divided; these things would not be good for his people and would not be advantageous to Jesus' purposes or kingdom. Jesus' prayer is an indication of his concern for the church. Jesus understands quite well the nature of the conflict that his people are engaged in. Light is battling darkness. While the battle frequently rages in the natural realm, it has its root in the spiritual realm. Jesus takes the battle very seriously; he addresses it in prayer, and his prayer is focused on God's provision for his people. Jesus does not want his people to buckle under to the opposition that the enemy brings to the church. This opposition can take many forms; it can come in the form of persecution, sickness, or, a major concern of this prayer, division. The enemy knows that pressure and a sense of being isolated can do much to undermine the work of the kingdom, and so he will do all he can to bring these things to bear upon the church. Jesus expresses care for his people by praying that they will not fall prey to these pitfalls.

The Importance of Unity

Unity among the people of God is very important; this can be seen from Jesus' prayer in John 17 and from other texts as well. Jesus is not the only one concerned about unity; unity was also a major concern of the apostle Paul (Rom 16:17–18; 1 Cor 1:10; Eph 4:3; Phil 1:27; Titus 3:10). As the previously mentioned Scripture references indicate, Paul wrote about unity to Christian people in a number of different locations. There are some very practical reasons why unity is so important. People cannot walk together unless they are agreed (Amos 3:3), and a house divided against itself cannot stand (Mark 3:25); disunity disturbs the sense of peace and well-being. Unity is also important because more can be accomplished when people work together than when they work independently or are separated from one another. These things should make it clear that unity is both desirable and necessary for the people of God.

God has also demonstrated that he blesses his people when they are united. He blessed the disciples in the early church after they gathered together for ten days in united prayer; God poured out the Holy Spirit on them (Acts 1:14; 2:1–4). The Lord also blessed a united church later in the book of Acts. After the healing of the man at the Gate Beautiful in Acts 3, Peter and John were taken before the Sanhedrin. The Sanhedrin threatened the apostles and told them not to speak or teach in the name of Jesus anymore (Acts 4:18). When the apostles were released, they went back to the church (Acts 4:23). The church lifted their voices together to God, and God answered their prayer in a powerful way, filling all who were gathered there with the Holy Spirit so that they could carry on the work of God in spite of the threats of the Sanhedrin (Acts 4:24–31). In Acts 12, we find that the apostle Peter was put in prison (Acts 12:3–5). This was a source of great concern to the other believers, and they earnestly prayed to God for him (Acts 12:5); this resulted in Peter's release from prison (Acts 12:7–10).

However, in John 17, Jesus' concern about unity is focused not so much on the benefit that unity will be to his followers as on the effect that unity will have on people who are outside of the community of faith. Jesus prayed that his people would be united so that the world would know and believe that the Father sent him into the world (John 17:23, 21). If the church is united, it can do much to help people be receptive to Jesus Christ; if the church does not demonstrate unity, it may actually keep people from coming to faith in Christ. The church's behavior can work at cross purposes with the mission that Jesus gave her to do (Matt 28:18–20). In 1995, Dr. John Stott spoke at a large Christian conference in Boston; the theme of the conference was "Woven Together . . . So the World May Know." As he spoke in the Hynes Auditorium, Dr. Stott said, "The world's belief depends on our behavior."[2] This is a sobering thought. The mission of the church in the world is somehow tied into this matter of unity. Unity is important to the church in order that she may be strong and vibrant, and it is important to the world. Unity, or the lack of it, affects the openness of unbelievers to Jesus Christ and thus their eternal destiny. The stakes are very high. Will we answer the prayer of Jesus or not? Will we, as the church, be united? A number of years ago, my friend and former pastor, Rev. John King, gave a teaching at a denominational meeting in New York City. He wrote the word *unity* on the board and pointed out that the word contained the letters *u* and *i*. He said that unity is about "you" and "I," and it is.

---

2. Stott, plenary session of the Evangelistic Association of New England's Congress, 1995.

A WORKING DEFINITION OF UNITY

Before talking further about unity, it is necessary to define how the word *unity* will be used in this book. The word *unity* surely means different things to different people. As I attempt to define how the word is used in this book, I will start by stating first what I do *not* mean by unity. As others before me have pointed out, unity does not mean uniformity. Unity does not mean that the entire body of Christ is going to become one large denomination that agrees on every point of doctrine and practice. Differences in doctrine, worship style, church government, and other things will surely continue to exist until Jesus returns. In this book, I use the word *unity* to mean the essential cooperation of born-again believers, regardless of denominational affiliation, working together for kingdom purposes. This unity is predicated on the acceptance of certain cardinal doctrines of the faith: the nature of God (this would include the doctrine of the Trinity), the inspiration and authority of Scripture, the person and work of Jesus Christ, and the necessity of a born-again experience. These are foundational truths on which all genuine believers ought to be able to agree. Churches and believers that hold to these basic beliefs should be able to work together. Ministries in which Christians might work together include evangelism, prayer, and mercy ministries such as the providing of food and clothing to those in need. All of these are ministries that have biblical foundations (Matt 28:18–20; Acts 2:42; Matt 25). Unity can bring much glory to the Lord, both through its testimony to the unbelieving world and through the work that is actually accomplished through cooperative efforts.

2

Examples of Disunity in the New Testament Church

T HE BIBLE DECLARES THAT there is "one Lord, one faith, one baptism; one God and Father of all, who is over all and through all and in all" (Eph 4:5–6). Even though all of these things are true, having and maintaining unity was a challenge for the early Christians; this can clearly be seen in the pages of the New Testament. In chapter 1, I cited a few biblical texts in which the disciples of Jesus demonstrated disunity (Mark 9:34; Luke 22:24; Mark 10:35–41), but Jesus' earliest followers were not the only offenders; those who believed their preaching were also at times not unified. There are many texts that indicate that the early Christians sometimes struggled with the issue of unity. In this chapter we will do a brief survey of some of these texts. This survey will not be exhaustive, but merely representative; nonetheless, it will demonstrate that unity was a challenge for the first-century followers of Jesus. The focus of our survey will be the book of Acts, the epistles, and the letters to the seven churches in Revelation chapters 2 and 3. The history of Acts, the directives of the epistles, and the narratives of the letters to the seven churches will show that unity was difficult for the first-century Christians to have and maintain. We turn our attention first to the book of Acts.

THE BOOK OF ACTS

The book of Acts records the early history of the Christian church; it covers a time period of about 30 years as Christianity spread from Judea to the city of Rome.[1] As this history unfolds, the problems that arose in the infant church are not omitted; they are included in the biblical text. As we survey some of the passages that are relevant to the discussion of unity, we will see that the errors and shortcomings of both church members and church leaders are included.

Acts 6

The first five chapters of the book of Acts depict a church that is flourishing. There was great unity (Acts 1:14; 2:42–45; 4:32–35); phenomenal growth (Acts 2:41, 47; 4:4; 5:14); and many miracles were taking place (Acts 2:43; 3:6–8; 5:16). The church enjoyed the favor of God and of the people (Acts 2:47). During this time the church did encounter a challenge from the outside; the Sanhedrin put pressure on Peter and John to stop talking about Jesus (Acts 4:17–21). Apart from this and the incident of hypocrisy involving Ananias and Sapphira, the church seems to have been pretty much at peace. In Acts 6 we find the church facing a significant challenge from among its own numbers.

The church was growing; as it did, it began to help take care of widows (Acts 6:1). This development is not surprising. In the Old Testament, God instructed his people to take care of widows (Deut 26:12). Since the church at this time was almost exclusively Jewish, it was quite natural for the believers to continue this practice as a part of their faith. We are not told when or how the Jerusalem church began its ministry to widows. When we come to Acts 6, the ministry is already up and running. However, there was a problem. Some of the Grecian Jews were complaining against the Hebraic Jews that their widows were not being taken care of in the daily distribution to the widows. The issue in this

1. Bruce, *Acts*, 20.

situation was two-fold; it was a justice issue and an ethnic issue. It was a justice issue because there was an alleged inequality in care, a partiality or favoritism. It was also an ethnic issue. While all of the widows were Jewish, they came from different places. The Hebraic Jews were those who hailed from the land of Israel; the Grecian Jews were probably those who hailed from outside of Palestine but had settled in Jerusalem.[2] They would be Diaspora Jews, Jews of the dispersion. The allegation of inequity feeds into the ethnic issue because the alleged favoritism appeared to have been divided along the ethnic lines mentioned above. We do not know how many people were affected by this situation, but the issue was significant enough to come to the attention of the apostles. This problem caused disunity in the church; it could have divided it if the situation had not been properly dealt with.

Acts 11

In Acts 10, through a series of divinely orchestrated circumstances, the apostle Peter brought the gospel to the household of Cornelius. God sent an angel to Cornelius to instruct him to send for Peter (Acts 10:3–6) who would give him a message whereby he and his household would be saved (Acts 11:14). God also dealt with Peter through a vision (Acts 10:10–16) and the voice of the Holy Spirit (Acts 10:19) in order to get Peter to go to the house of Cornelius. Bringing the gospel to the household of Cornelius was very significant; it was significant because Cornelius was a Gentile (Acts 10:28). All of those who had gathered at Cornelius' house became Christians when they heard Peter preach about Jesus Christ. As Acts 11 opens, we find that the news about what had happened at Cornelius' house had spread; the apostles and believers throughout Judea heard that the Gentiles had received the word of God (Acts 11:1). This preaching of the good news did not initially seem like good news to some. Acts 11:2 tells us that when Peter returned to Jerusalem he was criticized for going to

---

2. Keener, *Bible Background Commentary*, 338.

Cornelius' house. The issue here seems to be both cultural and theological. It is cultural in that Peter ate with, or had fellowship with, Gentiles who were ritually unclean (Acts 11:2).[3] We, in the West, do not typically think of eating with someone as being especially significant, but in New Testament times it was a sign of acceptance.[4] Peter's actions indicated that he accepted the Gentiles. This incident was also theological in that there were questions at this point in church history about non-Jews who came to faith in Jesus. The gospel had already reached the Samaritans (see Acts 8) in keeping with Jesus' words in Acts 1:8, but now it had reached full-blooded Gentiles. The church was predominantly Jewish at this time, and so "others" (non-Jews) made some Jewish believers uncomfortable. The division in this text was short-lived, but I include it here because it involved one of the leaders of the early church. Peter, who was one of the original apostles, was at odds with a number of people from the Jerusalem church. Some of those who criticized him were probably his fellow apostles (Acts 11:1–3). Peter's actions drove a bit of a wedge into the relationship between Peter and the other Jewish believers. This situation had the potential of becoming a source of division for the early church. The issue could have divided the leadership of the church as Jewish opinion and Peter's experience of divine direction pulled in opposite directions.

Acts 15—The Jerusalem Council

We saw in the previous section that in Acts 10, in a landmark case, the apostle Peter took the gospel to the Gentiles. As we proceed through the book of Acts, we find that others also brought the gospel to the Gentiles. Acts 11:19 tells us that some who left Jerusalem as result of the persecution that arose after the stoning of Stephen shared the gospel with non-Jews. We see ministry to Gentiles most notably in the missionary work of Paul and

3. Ibid., 353.
4. Ibid., 231.

Barnabas in Acts chapters 13 and 14. More and more Gentiles were coming to faith in Jesus Christ. This situation caused concern, and division, in the early church. There were some people who were teaching that Gentile men who put their faith in Jesus had to be circumcised (Acts 15:1); the issue became a crisis in Antioch. There was such contention over the matter that a council was held in Jerusalem to resolve the issue. The leadership of the Christian Church, specifically the apostles and elders, met to discuss the matter (Acts 15:6). Paul and Barnabas did not agree with the "circumcision" view (Acts 15:2). In fact, their disagreement with those who expressed it was quite strong; it is described as having been "sharp" (Acts 15:2). Unlike the situation concerning the widow's distribution in Acts 6, which only affected the church in Jerusalem, the issue considered at the Jerusalem Council had affected a number of churches and could potentially have affected the entire Christian movement. The substance of the issue in this dispute was theological. Can non-Jewish people, specifically men, be saved simply by believing in Jesus Christ, or must they also be circumcised and obey the Law of Moses (Acts 15:1, 5)? Representatives of both sides of the issue were in attendance at the council and presented their cases (Acts 15:5–12). During the course of the proceedings, there was disagreement, discussion, and finally decision. Of all the cases that we have looked at so far, this is the one that posed the greatest threat to the church; it could have seriously divided the whole Christian movement.

Acts 15—Paul and Barnabas

We have already seen one case in which a spiritual leader was involved in a brief situation of disunity. In Acts 11, we saw that the apostle Peter was "called on the carpet" by some people in the Jerusalem church, because he had gone to the home of Cornelius, who was a Gentile, and had eaten with him. In Acts 15:36–40 we find two spiritual leaders who had worked extensively with each other at odds with one another. The two people that I am referring to are Paul and Barnabas, both of whom were apostles

(Acts 14:14). Barnabas had "opened the door of the church" to the newly saved Saul of Tarsus (Paul). After Saul encountered Jesus on the Damascus Road and had become a believer, he tried to join the other believers in Jerusalem. The church at that time was not convinced of the sincerity of his Christian faith (Acts 9:26). Barnabas, however, believed him and took him to the apostles; after Barnabas spoke on his behalf Saul (Paul) was accepted by the church.

After this incident, Paul and Barnabas worked with each other on a number of occasions. The two of them taught the church in Antioch for a year (Acts 11:26), went on a missionary journey together (Acts 13 and 14), and revisited some of the cities that they had been to on their first missionary journey in order to strengthen the believers and set elders in the churches (Acts 14:21–23). They also participated together in the Jerusalem Council (Acts 15:2, 12). Paul and Barnabas had a significant history with one another; they had traveled together, taught together, and labored together for the same cause.

In Acts 15, we find them fighting with each other. Luke describes their disagreement as "sharp" (Acts 15:39). Their disagreement was not doctrinal or cultural; it concerned a person— John Mark. John Mark had accompanied Paul and Barnabas on part of their first missionary journey. Though we do not know exactly why, at some point during the trip John Mark left the team and returned to the city of Jerusalem (Acts 13:13). When Paul and Barnabas were about to go out on another ministry trip, Barnabas wanted to take John Mark along with them, but Paul did not because he had left them on their first missionary journey (Acts 13:13). The two of them could not agree on him, so they parted company over the matter.

Acts 20

In Acts 20:17–37, we find the apostle Paul ministering to the elders of the church of Ephesus. Paul was in the city of Miletus, and he sent for the elders and asked them to join him there. When they arrived, he began to speak to them. During the course of his speaking, he reminded them of how he had conducted himself in ministry in Ephesus, told them what the Spirit was indicating awaited him in Jerusalem, and gave them instructions concerning the ministry. He charged them to be faithful in their ministry (Acts 20:28) and warned them of coming troubles (Acts 20:29). One of the things he told them was that there would be some who would arise from within the church who would distort the truth and draw away disciples after themselves (Acts 20:30). At the time that Paul spoke these words the situation that he described had not yet taken place. In fact, Paul said that it would take place after he left (Acts 20:29). It seems that this word was fulfilled shortly thereafter, as the situation described in 1 Timothy (which was addressed to Timothy who was in the church in Ephesus) sounds very much like what Paul warned the Ephesian elders about in Acts 20.[5] The dividing line here was the issue of truth; the underlying reason for the division was false doctrine. This situation did prove to be problematic for the church in Ephesus.

THE EPISTLES

The New Testament epistles were written primarily to offer the new Christian congregations instruction, encouragement, and correction. Each epistle was an "occasional document"; this means that each epistle was written to address the specific needs of the church in a given location.[6] The epistles were in some sense "tailor-made" for each church. In these writings we also find evidence that the early church struggled to have, and maintain, unity. In this section we will look at a sampling of verses from the epistles that indicate that unity was in some sense challenged or broken in a number of the apostolic churches.

---

5. Fee, *1 & 2 Timothy, Titus*, 7.

6. Fee & Stuart, *How to Read the Bible*, 48.

Romans

The apostle Paul did not start the church in Rome. It may have been started by Romans who had been in Jerusalem and heard Peter preach on the first Christian Pentecost.[7] At the time of the writing of this epistle, Paul had not yet visited the church in Rome (Rom 1:10; see also 15:23). Even though he had not been to the church, he seems to have some knowledge of what was going on there. In the epistle there are hints that there was some conflict, or differences of opinion, among the believers on a number of things. These issues seem to be between Jewish and Gentile believers who, because of culture, expressed their faith differently.[8] Evidence of this conflict can be seen in the extensive discussions concerning Jews and Gentiles in the opening chapters of the epistle. Another hint of ethnic friction in the Roman church can be found in chapter 11 where Paul addresses the Gentiles in the church and urges them not to be too boastful or arrogant (see Rom 11:17—21, 25) because they have been grafted into a Jewish root.[9] Paul sought to keep the Jewish believers from becoming too proud earlier in the epistle (Rom 2:17—3:20). Further evidence of conflict can be found in Romans 14. In this chapter we find discussions about foods and holy days; both of these things would be issues that Jewish and Gentile people might disagree about.[10] The Jewish believers may have insisted on eating "clean" foods and the observance of the Sabbath as the day of worship.[11] Gentile believers would probably not have felt that either of these was crucial. Ethnic differences between these two groups were apparently causing some friction. Paul, in his writing, tried to resolve some of the difficulty through the teaching that he presented in the epistle.

7. Elwell andYarbrough, eds., *Encountering the New Testament*, 276.
8. Keener, *Bible Background Commentary*, 412.
9. Wilson, *Our Father Abraham*, 12.
10. Keener, *Bible Background Commentary*, 442.
11. Ibid., 443.

1 Corinthians

The church in Corinth was severely fractured by division. This was in some measure a by-product of the ethos of the larger culture which included public boasting and self promotion; the Corinthians were bringing "the world" into the church.[12] I dare say that this church is the classic case of division (every pastor's nightmare). Paul, who was absent from Corinth, had heard of their problems. In the first chapter of this epistle he writes these words: "I appeal to you, brothers and sisters, in the name of our Lord Jesus Christ, that all of you agree with one another in what you say and that there be no divisions among you, but that you be perfectly united in mind and in thought. My brothers and sisters, some from Chloe's household have informed me that there are quarrels among you" (1 Cor 1:10–11). Their divisions can be seen in a number of places in the epistle. In chapter 1 we find that there was contention about the different ministers, in chapter 6 we learn that the Corinthians had lawsuits with one another, in chapters 11–14 we see that they exhibited disorder in public worship in their observance of communion and the exercise of spiritual gifts, and in chapter 15 we find that there was some division concerning the doctrine of the resurrection.[13] Their quarrels regarding the various Christian ministers were not something that the ministers had themselves promoted or contributed to (1 Cor 3:4–9; 4:1).[14] Their lawsuits with one another betrayed the fact that they were not acting in Christian love. The apparent abuse of the poor at the communion table also points to division in the church (1 Cor 11:17–22).[15] In addition, their lack of love is also seen in their relationships in the body regarding spiritual gifts: "I don't need you!" (1 Cor 12:21). They were a divided church; Paul said that this church was worldly (1 Cor 3:3).

---

12. Witherington, *Conflict & Community in Corinth*, 8.

13. Gutherie, *New Testament Introduction*, 440.

14. Fee, *Corinthians*, 130.

15. Ibid., 534–45.

Ephesians

It has been said that the epistle to the Ephesians is an epistle that does not seem to address a crisis in the church.[16] That may be true, but the epistle does offer some instructions that are pertinent to the subject of unity. The fact that these verses are included indicates that having, or maintaining, unity can be a problem for God's people at times. Consider the following texts.

In Ephesians 2:14 Paul makes the point that God has ". . . made the two one . . ." The two referred to in this passage are Jews and Gentiles.[17] The "dividing wall of hostility" may be a reference to the wall of partition found in the Temple that kept Jews and Gentiles apart.[18] This passage could disarm the potential of division based on ethnicity. In Ephesians 4:3 Paul writes, "Make every effort to keep the unity of the Spirit through the bond of peace." This admonition would not be necessary if unity was not at times challenged. In Ephesians 4:31–32 we find these words: "Get rid of all bitterness, rage and anger, brawling and slander, along with every form of malice. Be kind and compassionate to one another, forgiving each other, just as in Christ God forgave you." The fact that Paul offers these instructions indicates that Christians can sometimes exhibit these sinful behaviors. If they are left unchecked, they will very likely create disunity. The call to submit to one another in Ephesians 5:21 is also good counsel to help prevent disunity.

Philippians

Philippians is one of the epistles that Paul wrote from prison; this is clear from his repeated references to "chains" (Phil 1:7,13–14, 17). This epistle too has texts that indicate that there was some unrest in the church.[19] For example, Paul's imperative in Philippians

---

16. Snodgrass, *Ephesians*, 22.

17. Keener, *Bible Background Commentary*, 544.

18. Ibid.

19. Fee, *Philippians*, 29.

1:27–28.[20] In this text he tells the Philippians to be united in spirit and to work together for the gospel. These instructions seem to suggest that at that time they were not unified. Another text that seems to indicate that there was a problem with disunity is Philippians 2:1–4.[21] In view of this Paul gives the Philippians some directives to follow. One of the clearest indications that there was a problem with unity in the church is Philippians 2:2. In this verse Paul urges them to be "like-minded" and to be "one in spirit and purpose." A very clear indication of conflict in the church is also found in Philippians 4:2. While this was not a large-scale problem, it could potentially affect the whole church. In this verse we learn that there were two women in the church who were not getting along with one another. These women had worked together with Paul in the cause of the gospel. Paul urged one whom he called "my true companion" to help them to be reconciled. The text offers some evidence that these two women in Philippi were ministers.[22]

The Thessalonian Epistles

The church in Thessalonica, located in Macedonia, was a church that the apostle Paul founded on his second missionary journey (see Acts 17:1–9). Paul's coworkers on this journey were Silas and Timothy. The contents of the two epistles reveal a church that appears to be prospering in the Lord. They received the gospel in the midst of adverse circumstances (1 Thess 1:6) and were still living in difficult times (1 Thess 3:2–3; 2 Thess 1:4), yet in the midst of this they were "model" Christians to all of the believers in Macedonia and Achaia (1 Thess 1:7; 2 Thess 1:4). Paul says much in these epistles to commend the believers in Thessalonica. At the time when he wrote they were living in a way that pleased God (1 Thess 4:1), and he commended them for their faith and

---

20. Ibid.
21. Ibid., 177.
22. Keener, *Paul, Women & Wives*, 242–43.

love (1 Thess 3:6–7; 4:9–10; 2 Thess 1:3). He also acknowledged the fruits of their faith, hope, and love (1 Thess 1:3), and their tremendous evangelistic influence (1 Thess 1:8). Paul urged the disciples in Thessalonica to continue to excel in the Christian virtue of love (1 Thess 4:10). By and large the believers in Thessalonica seem to be a spiritually healthy group.

There are, however, a couple of hints in the epistles that there was some disunity in the church. The first problem is hinted at in 1 Thessalonians 5:14. In this verse Paul gave the church instructions to warn the idle. In the second epistle we get some more information about this. In 2 Thessalonians 3:6–15 we find that there were some in the Thessalonian church who had stopped working. While we are not told explicitly why, one possible explanation was that they felt that the Lord was returning soon, and so there was no need to work.[23] Whatever the reason, Paul was in essence telling them to "get back to work."

Another indication that there was some division, or potential division, in the church is hinted at in 1 Thessalonians 5:12–13. In these verses Paul instructs the church to respect their leaders and to live in peace with each other. These instructions would seem to indicate that there was some friction between the leaders of the church and some of the members of the congregation. The exact nature of this tension is not spelled out in the text.

The Epistles to Timothy

At the time Paul wrote these epistles to Timothy he was in the church in the city of Ephesus (1 Tim 1:3). The church in Ephesus was founded by the apostle Paul; the record of its beginning can be found in Acts 19. Ephesus was a city steeped in the occult (Acts 19:18–19), and Paul spent a considerable amount of time in this city when he planted the church there (see Acts 19:10). Prior to the writing of these epistles Paul had warned the elders of the church of Ephesus that there would be problems

23. Stott, *The Gospel & the End of Time*, 188–89.

in the church (Acts 20:29–31) that would come from inside the church itself. Specifically, the problems would involve false teaching and false teachers.

When Paul wrote these epistles, Timothy was dealing with this very thing; false teaching and false teachers were plaguing the church. The substance of these aberrant teachings, while not clearly laid out, contained Jewish and possibly Gnostic elements involving myths (and genealogies), misuses of the Old Testament Law, and prohibitions concerning food and marriage.[24] Proof of this can be found in many places in the epistles (1 Tim 1:3–4, 6–7; 4:1–7). Paul was in prison at this time and could not personally attend to the needs and problems of the Ephesian church. He had Timothy in the church to try to bring it back on course doctrinally.

James

The epistle of James may be the first written document of the New Testament.[25] It is believed that James, the Lord's brother, wrote it.[26] The epistle was written to Jewish believers in Jesus who lived in various locations in the first-century world (Jas 1:1). The book contains a lot of instructions about how one should live as a follower of Jesus. This epistle also hints at the fact that there were problems with disunity among the believers to whom it was sent.

One problem that we can see in this epistle is that of favoritism or partiality. The Bible is very clear that God is not partial (Rom 2:11; Eph 6:9); as children of God, we are not to be partial either, for we are all one in Christ Jesus (Gal 3:26–28; Col 3:11). The recipients of this letter apparently had not grasped this truth, and so James wrote to them concerning this matter. In James 1:9–10, he gave them some instruction to "level the ground." He

---

24. Barrett, *The Pastoral Epistles*, 12–13.

25. Walvoord and Zuck, eds., *The Bible Knowledge Commentary*, 816.

26. Keener, *Bible Background Commentary*, 686.

instructed the humble believer to take pride in his elevated position in Christ and the rich believer to be humble. If both parties heeded this instruction, it would do much to help them relate to each other as members of one body. In James 2 the problem of partiality is directly addressed. This passage shows that the partiality had to do with showing preferential treatment to the rich. James told the recipients of the epistle that this was not right.

There are also other indications of division or disunity in this epistle. In chapter 4 James wrote about fights and quarrels (4:2). The language here is that of conflict; conflict is not conducive to unity. Evidence of division can also be seen in the last chapter of the epistle as James instructed the believers not to grumble against one another (Jas 5:9). Evidently the personal relationships between some of the believers were not what God would have them to be.

All of these texts indicate that there were problems in the congregations addressed in this epistle; there was tension and conflict in the churches. The unity of the congregations was fractured, and James sought to remedy these situations.

The Letters to the Seven Churches in Revelation 2 and 3

It does not appear that all seven of the churches addressed in Revelation 2 and 3 suffered from division, but there is evidence that some of them did. In chapter 2 we find that the church in Pergamum had a problem; their problem concerned doctrine. There were at least two forms of aberrant teaching affecting the church. There were some in the church who held to the teaching of Balaam (Rev 2:14), and some who held to the teachings of the Nicolaitans (Rev 2:15). Whatever the content of these two teachings was Jesus was not pleased with them, and he told the church to repent, to turn away from these teachings, and to return to sound teaching. Bad doctrine inevitably leads to bad behavior.

The church in Thyatira also had a unity problem, and like the church in Pergamum, it was also a doctrinal problem. The church in Thyatira was tolerating the ministry of a self-proclaimed prophetess, Jezebel (Rev 2:20). The church allowed her to carry on her "ministry" unchecked; this displeased Jesus, and he informed the church that he was going to deal with them.

The church in Sardis was also not united. Most of the believers there were spiritually asleep and were displeasing to the Lord (Rev 3:2, 4). There was, however, a remnant who did apply themselves spiritually, and Jesus was pleased with them (Rev 2:4).

THE BOTTOM LINE

This chapter demonstrates that there are many things that can separate believers from one another, and no one is exempt. In this survey we have seen leaders divided from one another, churches at odds with their leaders, and congregations divided amongst themselves. There were many reasons for these divisions. Some of the division was a result of church growth, some was due to matters of culture or ethnicity, and others were because of theological understanding, false doctrine, and partiality. All of these things get in the way of believers working together because when people do not agree with each other they typically will not walk together (Amos 3:3). As Jesus said, " . . . a house divided against itself will fall" (Luke 11:17). If division will cause a fall, such a "house" will not be effective in working for the kingdom. The obstacles that we have seen in this chapter may seem quite formidable and difficult to overcome. This raises the question, "Why is it so difficult to have and maintain unity?" I will seek to answer that question in the next chapter.

3

Why Is It So Difficult?

"MAKE EVERY EFFORT TO keep the unity of the Spirit through the bond of peace" (Eph 4:3). The verse I just cited was written by the apostle Paul, and it is a very interesting one. It is interesting because of what it implies; it implies that there is a built-in unity that God has given to believers. If this were not so, then we could not make efforts to maintain it. To maintain is to seek to continue something which is already in place. It is clear from Scripture that God has given believers a basis for unity. Those who are truly born again are all children of God in Christ Jesus (Gal 3:26) and are all partakers of one Spirit (Rom 8:9; Eph 1:13). Thus, our unity is in the Lord, and God has given us this unity. Another truth that we can glean from Ephesians 4:3 is that this unity will be challenged. If we are called to *maintain* unity, then it is likely that unity can deteriorate into disunity. In addition to indicating that our unity in Christ will be challenged, this verse also teaches that each believer has a responsibility to take steps to preserve this unity that the Lord has given. Since the text was addressed to the church as a whole, all believers bear this responsibility; it is not the sole responsibility of the leadership of the church. Unity will not continue to exist for any great length of time without our conscious attempts to guard and keep it. You might say, "Why not? God has given us unity, right?" Yes, the Lord has, but there are forces that militate against what God desires. The forces that I am speaking about come from both outside and inside the church.

They are the world, the flesh or sinful nature, and the devil. Let us now briefly consider each of these.

THE WORLD

The first challenge to unity that we will look at comes from outside of the church. I am referring to what we call *the world*. Some people might take the term *the world* to mean the planet earth, and in some texts that is what it does mean (John 17:11; Acts 17:24; Eph 1:4). However, when I speak of *the world* in this section, I am using a more narrow New Testament meaning of the term. Jesus and the apostles sometimes used the term *the world* to refer to the ways of the unbelieving or pagan world (Luke 12:30; 16:8; John 15:18–19; Rom 12:2; Jas 1:27; 4:4; 1 John 4:5). Paul described it as the spirit of the world (1 Cor 2:12). That is how I am using the term *the world* in this section.

If you have been in the church for any length of time, you have probably heard the expression that "the world has gotten into the church." In other words, something that does not belong in church has come in from the outside world. Worldliness means different things to different believers. Some think of worldliness in terms of external matters such as clothing, jewelry, and makeup. In some, though not all, cases these things can be worldly. If one is immodest or extreme with reference to these outward adornments, then they may very well be worldly. However, Paul seems to offer us a different understanding of what it means to be worldly.

In the book of 1 Corinthians Paul addressed a very troubled church in Corinth. In chapter 3 he wrote these words: "Brothers and sisters, I could not address you as spiritual but as worldly— mere infants in Christ. I gave you milk, not solid food, for you were not yet ready for it. Indeed, you are still not ready. You are still worldly. For since there is jealousy and quarreling among you, are you not worldly?" (1 Cor 3:1–3). In this passage Paul equates jealousy and quarreling with worldliness. This is a concept that for the most part the contemporary church has not recognized. The specific issue at hand in 1 Corinthians 3 was that various members of the congregation had pledged their allegiance to different ministers. In addition to quarreling, favoritism was also present in the church. The result: division.

This is not the only form of worldliness that can divide the people of God. One issue of major importance is the matter of forgiveness. If people refuse to offer and receive forgiveness, then there will be a sense of alienation and the unity of the church will suffer for it. Later in Ephesians Paul instructs the believers to be forgiving of one another (Eph 4:32). When offenses occur, reconciliation needs to be sought, and the quicker the better. Revenge, or "making the person pay," is not a biblical option. Revenge and unforgiveness are worldly. Any sinful attitude or behavior that the unbelieving world accepts as normal can divide believers if it is brought into the church and allowed to continue. The church is not supposed to function on worldly principles; it is supposed to function according the principles of the word of God. If it fails to do so, the result will be division.

THE FLESH OR SINFUL NATURE

This next challenge to unity is closely related to the one we just considered above. This second challenge comes from inside the church; it comes from individual believers. Sometimes Christians are affected by outside influences (the world), and sometimes they are simply acting upon their own sinful nature. In either case, if the ungodly influence is not restrained, the result will be sin, and sin divides. We can see this in the Bible as early as the book of Genesis; we can see it in the experience of Adam and Eve. Their relationship with one another and with God suffered once they sinned. Alienation and division were the fruits of their act. This same pattern can be found right on through the rest of Scripture. Sin does indeed divide. While believers are called to be holy (1 Thess 4:7; 2 Tim 1:9; 1 Pet 1:15), they do not always live up to their calling. Paul's teaching in Galatians 5:16–26 shows us that a Christian can exhibit either the fruit of the Spirit or the

acts of the sinful nature. The factor that determines the differ-
ence is whether believers allow the Holy Spirit to control their
lives or whether they allow the sinful nature to dominate them.
Paul urged the believers in the churches of Galatia to "walk by
the Spirit" (Gal 5:16). If they followed Paul's instructions, then
they would not gratify their sinful nature. When you look at the
list of things that characterize the acts of the sinful nature, then
you can understand why Paul gives this counsel. The behaviors
that are listed in Galatians 5:19–21 do not sound good, and they
are not. If you look through the list, you will notice a number of
items that would be major challenges to unity. The items that I
am referring to are hatred, discord, jealousy, fits of rage, selfish
ambition, dissensions, factions, and envy. All of these things are
unity killers because they all speak of hostility in relationships.
Such things cannot be allowed to remain in the church if the
church is to be united. As the Spirit is the one who gives believers
unity (Eph 4:3), the Spirit is also the one who empowers them to
continue in unity.

Paul's directives in Galatians 5 were not idle instructions;
they were given because there was a need for them. Indeed there
is still a need for them today. Christians do, from time to time,
walk according to their sinful nature rather than by the Holy
Spirit. Ray Stedman, in his book *Authentic Christianity*, made the
observation that believers can be under the control of the Spirit
in most areas of their lives but have one area in which they are
not submitted to the Holy Spirit and His control.[1] This is true,
and most Christians can testify to its truth by reflecting upon
their own experience as well as observing the behavior of others. There is evidence that there was unsanctified behavior in the
lives of some of the believers in the churches of the first century.
Passages such Ephesians 4:22–31 and Colossians 3:5–10 indicate
the presence of sinful attitudes and practices. These things must
be uprooted not only for the sake of personal holiness but also
for the health of the body because they cause division. Specific

---

1. Stedman, *Authentic Christianity*, 94–95.

examples of sinful behavior in the New Testament church that caused division include the unresolved conflict between Euodia and Syntyche (Phil 4:2) and Diotrephes' domineering control of the church that he was a part of (3 John 9–10).

THE DEVIL AND HIS WORKERS

The last challenge to the unity of the church that I will mention in this chapter comes from outside of the church. It is a wholly supernatural force—the devil and his workers. While some people, even Christians, may minimize their reality and power, the Bible portrays them as a very real force to be reckoned with. In Scripture, Satan, or the devil, is described as one who has power (Acts 26:18). He exerts his power in a number of different ways; the following are some of the ways that he works: he tempts (1 Cor 7:5); blinds (2 Cor 4:4); deceives (2 Cor 11:3; 1 Tim 2:14; Rev 20:10); outwits (2 Cor 2:11); masquerades as an angel of light (2 Cor 11:14); and blocks the way of believers (1 Thess 2:18). He is called a liar (John 8:44); the tempter (1 Thess 3:5); and the accuser of the brothers and sisters (Rev 12:10). This sampling of texts gives us a good idea of the kind of activities that the devil and his workers engage in. Perhaps the most graphic description of the believer's conflict with these forces is found in Ephesians 6:10–18.

The devil tries to drive a wedge between the believer and God to disrupt that relationship; he does this through temptations to sin. He also tries to drive a wedge between the relationships of believers; this he also does through enticements to sin. We are in a war with him, and he is using the military strategy "divide and conquer." Jesus said that a household divided against itself will not stand (Matt 12:25). The devil pits leaders against their congregations, congregations against their leaders, church members against each another, and churches against one another. As long as he can bring division, he is happy because it works toward his purposes and against God's purposes as expressed in Jesus' prayer in John 17. The devil will launch multiple attacks as he seeks to divide the people of God. He may hammer away in one area or exert pressure in a number of different areas. In his book, *The Spirit, The Church and the World,* John Stott says that the devil launched three attacks against the church in Jerusalem in the early chapters of Acts: his first attack was physical violence or persecution; his second attack was moral corruption, through the hypocrisy of Ananias and Sapphira; and his third attack was distraction evidenced by the problem concerning the aid for the widows in Acts 6.[2] Whether from without or within the enemy seeks to divide the church of Jesus Christ.

THE CHALLENGE OF THE CHALLENGES

The three challenges that I have listed in this chapter are very real, and they all are still very much with us today. Some of these challenges come from outside the church, and some of them come from inside. Since Paul tells us that we all have a responsibility to maintain the unity of the Spirit (Eph 4:3), Christians need to be aware of these challenges and watch out for them. When we detect one of them arising, we need to do all that we can to circumvent it. If we find that the world's ways are infiltrating our fellowship, we need to go back and study what the Bible says about how people should conduct themselves in the church of God (1 Tim 3:15). Knowledge of scriptural truth is an important starting point, but we need to move beyond; we need to take the next step to obedience. If we find that our sinful nature flares up, then we need to address that. This may entail apologizing to someone or praying for God's help to get victory over our sin. We may have to do both of these things. If things are being stirred up in the midst of our church, we need to ask ourselves if this is the enemy at work. This is sometimes difficult to determine because the enemy does, at times, work through people. If we sense that the conflict or disruption is demonic in nature, we need to guard against helping him; that is, we need to refrain from attacking one another. Christians are fighting a war on more than

2. Stott, *The Spirit, the Church and the World*, 105.

one front. This is not an easy thing to do. All of the things that we have looked at in this chapter are challenges to unity in the church. Unfortunately these are not the only challenges. There are other challenges that the church must come to terms with. In the next chapter we will look at some additional challenges to unity. Many of these challenges did not exist in the days of the first-century church but came into being over the course of church history. These challenges too can be hindrances to unity in a local congregation, but they are most definitely challenges to unity between Christians and Christian churches.

4

Additional Challenges to Unity

"MOURN AND WEEP, FOR the body of my son is broken."[1] The words that you have just read were part of a prophecy that was given at the Charismatic Conference of 1977 that was held in Kansas City, Missouri. This was a historic conference in that it brought together "The Three Streams"—the Classical Pentecostals, the Neo-Pentecostals, and the Catholic Pentecostals.[2] Thus, leaders and representatives from Catholic, Protestant, and Pentecostal backgrounds were gathered together in one place. That in itself qualifies as a miracle! Despite the diversity and differences of the groups represented, they came together around the Lordship of Christ and the work of the Holy Spirit. A record of the events of this conference can be found in the book *Like a Mighty River*.[3]

The words of the prophetic message, mentioned above, are very true. The body of Jesus, the church, is broken; it is fractured and fragmented in many ways. A quick look through Frank Mead's book *Handbook of Denominations in the United States* will demonstrate that.[4] There are literally hundreds of Christian denominations; in addition, there are also many independent churches that are not a part of any denomination. In this chapter

1. Manuel, *Like a Mighty River*, 195.

2. Ibid., 18.

3. Ibid.

4. Mead, *Handbook of Denominations in the United States.*

we are going to look at some more things that can breed disunity. The things that we will consider here can be stumbling blocks to unity in the local congregation or between Christian churches, and some can be problematic in both areas. Let us now turn our attention to these other impediments to unity.

THE CHALLENGES OF PEOPLE

In the New Testament one of the words that is used to refer to believers in Jesus is the word *saints* (see, for example, Rom 1:7; Eph 1:15; 3:18; Phil 4:22 NIV). This word is not reserved for a special, elite class of super holy Christians. Biblically speaking, it is a term used for all the followers of Jesus. With that said, I would like to share a little rhyme that is found in Ray Stedman's classic book, *Body Life*. This rhyme is cute and very true. In fact, it may be closer to home than we would like to admit:

> To dwell above with saints we love,
> Oh that will be glory.
> But to live below, with saints we know;
> Well, that's a different story![5]

We do at times have difficulty relating to one another in the body of Christ. We have all been saved through the blood of Jesus and are all partakers of the Holy Spirit, and yet in spite of these things we sometimes struggle with getting along. In his commentary on the book of Philippians, Warren Wiersbe notes that in chapter 1 of the epistle Paul says that he has the Philippians on his mind and in his heart; Wiersbe also notes that someone has pointed out that some believers would have to confess that they have others on their nerves.[6] Why is this so? What are some of the reasons for these tensions? I am sure that I do not know all of the answers, but the list below contains things that could certainly be challenges on the road to unity. Let us

---

5. Stedman, *Body Life*, 24–25.
6. Wiersbe, *The Bible Exposition Commentary*, 65.

first look at the people issues; after that, we will look at the issues of practice that divide us.

Age

The church is a very mixed group. One of the obvious differences is that of age, by which I mean biological age. The age range of people who attend church runs from newborns right on through to the elderly. In short, the church is a place for everybody. However, this dynamic can sometimes be problematic. Older members do not understand the ways of younger generations. Older members can sometimes be heard to make statements like, "Why do they want to change things? We have been doing things this way for decades. It has worked for us, why change it? It was good enough for us; why is it not good enough for them? This is our tradition; it is tried and true." They do not like the idea of change and may even think that the younger generation is departing from the truth (which in some cases may be true). On the other side of the equation, the younger generation can become impatient with older members. "They are so old-fashioned; they just don't understand. Times have changed." The younger generation can begin to speak and act as though older members do not know anything or have anything constructive to offer. As the various age groups pull in different directions, disunity can result.

Culture

People from different ethnic backgrounds or different parts of the world have varying ideas about what is acceptable. I can offer one example here. I once invited an international student from Singapore to speak at our church. When I picked him up that Sunday morning, he was dressed in a nice suit. He told me that when he originally got dressed that morning he did not put a suit on. He originally put on a pair of more casual pants and a tee shirt. He was dressing as he would if he were going to his church in Singapore. He caught himself that morning and remembered that he was not in Singapore but in the United States. He realized that the way he was accustomed to dressing might not be appreciated in our church. The way that he typically dressed for church in Singapore might not have been due just to ethnic culture. Though I don't know this for sure, it may also have been influenced by the youth culture of that country. When people of various cultures come together for worship, there is the potential for division. Some look upon the cultural differences of others, including issues such as clothing, as being inappropriate and disrespectful if they do not conform to the standards of the dominant culture in which the worship takes place.

Spiritual Maturity

The church is composed of people of different biological ages, and it is also composed of people who have different levels of spiritual maturity. There are a number of factors that contribute to the maturity of the believer: the length of time that they have been a Christian, the experiences of life that they have had, the opportunities that they have had for discipleship, and how much a person has applied him or herself to growing spiritually. In any local congregation there are people who are at different stages in their spiritual development. This can be a source of conflict and division. Those who are more mature can become impatient with the less mature. They can also become spiritually conceited. They can begin to consider themselves to be the "haves" and the others to be the "have nots." The less mature can either become defensive or wonder what the big deal is that is causing others to be upset with them. Patience can sometimes wear thin when people of varying degrees of spiritual maturity are gathered together as the people of God.

Spiritual Gifting

Spiritual gifting can also be a source of division. In his book, *Your Spiritual Gifts Can Help Your Church Grow,* C. Peter Wagner, mentions two abuses of spiritual gifts—gift exaltation and gift projection.[7] While Wagner was writing about church growth, seeking to foster it and remove obstacles to it, I think that the two abuses of spiritual gifts that he mentions also hold potential to foster disunity in the local church. Wagner describes gift exaltation as the exalting of one gift over the others.[8] If a person has this one exalted gift, they are a first-class citizen; if they do not, then they are a second-class citizen.[9] Gift projection is the idea that if you have a certain degree of consecration then you will be able to do the same things that others who have been greatly used by God have done.[10] These two abuses could wreck havoc in a church. Gift exaltation would have everyone seeking "the special gift" and would thereby downplay or dismiss the importance and contribution of other gifts. This would be detrimental to the spiritual health of the congregation since God has indicated that the exercise of the various spiritual gifts is necessary for the strengthening of the church (1 Cor 14:26). Gift projection could give everyone the idea that every member can do the same thing, and this is simply not true. Those who attempt to do so and fail will feel that there is something wrong in their relationship with God and could become discouraged or depressed.[11]

The Place of Men and Women in Ministry

We may not typically think of this as an issue that creates division, but it can. To my knowledge there is no branch of the Christian Church that questions which ministries a man may participate

7. Wagner, *Spiritual Gifts*, 45–48.

8. Ibid., 45.

9. Ibid.

10. Ibid., 46.

11. Ibid., 46–48.

in. Men can be worship leaders, deacons, and pastors. However, the issue of which ministries a woman may participate in is a different story. There are some in the church today who feel that women can participate in ministry, even teaching (as long as it is teaching other women or children), but that they cannot be pastors or in positions in which they would have authority over men. This is sometimes called the complementarian view; those who hold this view believe that there is a hierarchy with regard to men and women, with men holding the higher position.[12] Complementarians point to 1 Timothy 2:11–15 as a key text in support of their position.

There are others in the church who feel that women can participate in ministry on an equal basis with men. They do not believe that there is a hierarchy with reference to gender; they believe that a woman can be a pastor, even the senior pastor, and that she can exercise authority over a man; this view is commonly referred to as the egalitarian position.[13] Egalitarians point to texts such as Acts 18:26; Romans 16:1, 7; and Philippians 4:2–3 to support their view.

These two views stand at odds with one another. They are not just random opinions; they are based on certain doctrinal understandings. Both views point to various Scriptures to support their beliefs. If a church adopts the egalitarian view, there are some people who feel that the church has moved away from Scripture and has become liberal. If a church adopts the complementarian view, the women of that church may begin to feel like second-class citizens because this viewpoint excludes them from certain ministries. Living under these circumstances, the women will likely either leave the church or let some of their gifts go unused. Neither of these options contributes to the unity or benefit of the church.

12. Pierce and Groothuis, eds., *Discovering Biblical Equality*, 15.
13. Ibid.

Church Leaders

Church leaders can also be a cause for disunity. In some cases this is not their own fault; in other cases it is. For example, in 1 Corinthians Paul writes about people rallying around certain ministers, specifically they were rallying around Paul, Apollos, Cephas, and Christ (1 Cor 1:12). This division about the various leaders was in all likelihood not something that the leaders were party to.[14] This division was something that the people came up with themselves. Another example from the New Testament shows that a church can be divided because of the leader. In 3 John we read about a man named Diotrephes. From what we read about him in the epistle he seems to be a person with some authority in the church. As itinerant believers came his way, he would not welcome them, and he put out of the church those members who did want to assist them. The situation was so bad that the apostle John said that he was going to deal with it if he went there (3 John 10). Church leaders are supposed to foster unity (Eph 4:12–13), but they do not always do so.

SUMMARY OF THE PEOPLE CHALLENGES

Age, culture, spiritual maturity, spiritual gifting, the issue of the ministry of men and women in the church, and the influence of church leaders can all potentially disrupt unity in the local church. These issues could also be sources of conflict between specific churches. All of these things have to do with relationships—how people interact with one another. These are certainly matters to be reckoned with, but they are not the only challenges: various practices of the church can also be obstacles to unity. These practices can be issues that divide a local church, but they are more likely to keep Christians from different churches apart. We turn our attention now to these practices.

14. Fee, *Corinthians*, 55.

THE CHALLENGE OF PRACTICES

Every church or denomination has its own way of doing things or its own understanding of how things should be done. These differences are based on certain doctrinal understandings. In this section we are going to briefly look at some of the practices that currently divide the Christian Church. It should be noted that in some cases while we agree that certain practices *should* be done, we do not agree about *how* they should be done.

Water Baptism

Water baptism is mentioned in a number of places in the New Testament (Acts 2:38, 41; 8:12, 38; 9:18; 16:33). It was practiced by the early church because Jesus commanded it (Matt 28:19). Most, though not all, Christian churches and denominations believe that it is a practice that is meant to be carried on by the church today. However, we do not agree about how it should be administered. Should the baptismal candidate have the water sprinkled on them, poured over them, or should they be immersed in it? In addition to the mode by which baptism should be administered, should the person being baptized be an adult who has made his or her own profession of faith, or can the person be an infant who has someone else speak on its behalf? Those who believe in baptism by immersion do so, at least in part, because Acts 8:38 says that Philip and the Ethiopian Eunuch ". . . went down into the water . . ." when Philip baptized him. Because immersion requires putting the candidate totally under the water, advocates of baptism by immersion typically believe that a person must be old enough to be able to handle being totally immersed. They also believe that the person should make their own profession of faith prior to being baptized. This belief is thought to follow the New Testament pattern, first believe and then be baptized (Mark 16:16). Those who support the practice of sprinkling or pouring do not see immersion as necessary and tend to see baptism more as a sign of entrance or welcome into the community of faith, like circumcision in the Old Testament.[15]

Communion

Communion is an ordinance or sacrament of the church. It was established by Christ (Matt 26:26–29; Mark 14:22–25; Luke 22:19–20), and he gave instructions that it is to be practiced on an ongoing basis (1 Cor 11:23–26). We find evidence in the New Testament that the church did carry on the practice of communion as Jesus had instructed them to. One major text that deals with communion is 1 Corinthians 11:17–34. Other texts that may refer to communion are Acts 2:42 and Jude 12. In the verse in Acts 2 the reference to the breaking of bread suggest communion, though probably as part of a larger meal.[16] The love feast referred to in Jude 12 was another name for a meal that included partaking of communion.[17] Some church traditions use grape juice and bread to observe the ordinance; some use wafers or crackers in place of the bread. Others use wine and bread because wine was what was used in the Bible. While there is general agreement that communion ought to be practiced and that two elements are to be used, that is about as far as the agreement goes. There are differences as to the number of times that communion should be observed during the course of a year: some think it should be part of every Sunday service, others believe that it should be practiced once a month, and still others think that it should be practiced at lesser intervals. There are also differences of opinion as to what communion is. Roman Catholics believe that the elements really become the body and blood of Jesus; this is called "transubstantiation."[18] Some mainline Protestants believe that Christ is present in the communion; this is called "consubstantiation," that the body and

15. Erickson, *Christian Theology*, 1102–4.
16. Stott, *The Spirit, the Church and the World*, 84–85.
17. Keener, *Bible Background Commentary*, 755.
18. Erickson, *Christian Theology*, 1124.

blood of Christ are present in communion but that the partakers still have real bread and the wine.[19] Still other Christians believe that communion is only a commemoration of the death of Christ.[20] Some Christians believe that a person has to have been baptized in water in order to take communion, and others do not.[21]

The Wearing of Clerical Garments

My wife and I visited a class at Gordon-Conwell Theological Seminary that our friend, the Rev. Dr. Grace May, was teaching. The class was about women in ministry. In this class she asked the students, "If you are asked to speak at a church should you 'robe up?'" What she meant by this is should you put on vestments, clerical garb? The answer to this question depends on a couple of things. First, do you think that vestments are appropriate to wear? And second, and perhaps more importantly, does the church you are going to be ministering at think that special clothing is appropriate? If you have had the opportunity to visit a number of different church traditions, you will have noted that some churches use clerical garb and some do not. The presence or absence of this special clothing can communicate a couple of different things. Dr. May asked what a robe signifies. One person in the class said that it signified that the one wearing the robe was an authorized person. While this may be true, the wearing of a robe may also send a message to the person in the pew that they are not authorized to do ministry. If that happens, the expression of the priesthood of all believers will be hindered in that church. The priesthood of all believers is a term commonly used to refer to the biblical teaching that every Christian is to be involved in ministry. Scriptures which support this teaching include Ephesians 4:11–12; 1 Peter 4:10–11; Romans 12:6–8 and 1 Corinthians 12:1–11.

19. Ibid., 1125.
20. Ibid., 1128.
21. Ibid., 1122.

Worship

The people of God are meant to worship; there is no question about that. The Bible is replete with examples of, and instructions for, worship (Exod 23:25; Ps 29:2; 95:6; 100:2; Matt 4:10; John 4:23–24; Acts 13:2; 24:14; Rev 22:9). The question is what worship should look like. Should worship be liturgical? By that I mean should the service be very structured with responsive readings and everyone standing, sitting, and kneeling at the same time? Or should the service be more spontaneous with very little structure, just perhaps a general order of service which could be deviated from if the Lord moved in a particular way? Also, should worship be boisterous and joyful, or should it be quiet and restrained? Different church traditions tend to emphasize one or the other of these two models. Those who favor the liturgical type of service can point to Scripture in support of their preference. They can point to some of the organized worship of Israel and Paul's words in 1 Corinthians 14:40 that all things should be done in a decent and orderly way. Proponents of the less structured type of service can also point to Scripture in support of their practice. They can point to John 4:24 and Philippians 3:3 which speak about worshipping by the Spirit (who seems, at least at times, to be spontaneous). Those who prefer a quiet worship service may refer to Psalm 46:10 which tells us to be still and know that God is God; those who like a more boisterous service can refer to Psalm 47:1 which instructs worshipers to clap and shout. Closely related to this issue of worship is the subject of musical instruments. What musical instruments, if any, are appropriate for church? Should we use only a piano or organ, or can guitars and drums be used as well?

Church Government

Biblically speaking, Jesus Christ is the ultimate authority in the church (Eph 1:22; 4:15; 5:23; Col 1:18; 2:19). Even though this is true, every church still needs to have some form of human leadership. That is, every church needs to have people who make decisions and set policy for the congregation (hopefully in keeping with the will and Spirit of God as revealed in the Scriptures). Though the primary source book for all Christian churches is the Bible, not all are agreed as to where the authority of the church should rest. Some churches hold to a congregational form of government in which the people who make up the local congregation have a voice in what is done in the church. Those who have this type of government might appeal to Acts 6 where the congregation in Jerusalem decided who would take care of the distribution to the widows.

Other congregations hold to a very different form of government in which the pastor or elders govern the church. Those who support this model of government might appeal to texts like 1 Timothy 5:17 and Titus 1:5–9. Still other congregations blend these two forms of church government. The pastor or elders provide leadership or oversight in most areas concerning the church, but the congregation has a voice in some major decisions such as the acquisition or disposal of church property. In other denominational polity, some decisions affecting the congregation are made outside of the congregation and are passed on to local church leadership to be carried out.

SUMMARY OF THE PRACTICE CHALLENGES

The practices of the church—baptism, communion, the wearing or not wearing of clerical garments, worship, and church government—are all things that involve people, and they are all visible in the church. Differences in these areas are very obvious and can be stumbling blocks between churches. Churches who baptize only adult believers may distance themselves from those who baptize infants, those who do not wear clerical garments may feel uncomfortable around those who do, and those who use grape juice in communion may feel uncomfortable with churches that use wine. These are just a few examples of potential obstacles to unity. However, there is another area which is an even bigger challenge to unity, and that is the area of doctrine. We will now briefly look at some topics about which the Christian church has different viewpoints.

DOCTRINAL CHALLENGES

In the previous section we looked at practices that could be challenges to unity. Some of those practices are based on doctrinal understandings—for example, the practice of water baptism. But there are many other areas in which there is doctrinal disagreement among believers. These doctrinal differences may not immediately be visible when you enter a church, but they will eventually surface, and they can hold great power among the people there. These beliefs are matters of great doctrinal conviction. Accepting them indicates that you are orthodox, that you respect biblical authority. If you do not accept the particular doctrinal view of the church, you may be considered unorthodox (at least in the area in which you differ with the church's official doctrinal position). Below are just a few of the doctrinal differences that can be found among believers.

Salvation

All conservative Christians believe that their salvation is found in the person and work of Jesus Christ (John 3:16; 14:6; Acts 4:12; 1 Tim 2:5–6). They also believe that it is attained by grace through faith (Eph 2:8–9). However, there is a difference of opinion over "who found whom?" Did I find the Lord, or did he find me? That is, which is more important with regard to salvation, divine sovereignty or human free will? This is part of the Calvinist–Arminian debate. Those who hold to the Calvinistic viewpoint emphasize the importance of divine sovereignty while those who hold to the Arminian view emphasize the importance of human free will. Both views can marshal Scriptures to support their position. Calvinists point to verses like John 15:16, 19; Arminians appeal to texts like Romans 10:13.

Spiritual Gifts

There is no question that spiritual gifts existed in the days of the New Testament church. There were a number of different gifts in operation back then. The apostle Paul wrote about them in Romans 12 and 1 Corinthians chapters 12—14. The book of Acts also contains accounts of various gifts in operations, gifts like prophecy (Acts 11:27–28; 21:10–11), healing (Acts 3:6–8; 8:7; 9:17–18), and miracles (Acts 5:12; 19:11). There is some discussion in the contemporary church about which gifts are still in operation today. Charismatics and Pentecostals generally believe that all of the gifts that are mentioned in the New Testament are still in operation today.[22] There are other Christians who believe that the miraculous gifts of the Holy Spirit that we find mentioned in the New Testament no longer function today; these people are known as cessationists.[23] They usually hold to the belief that the gifts of tongues, prophecy, and healing were only for the first century and are no longer in operation.[24] Charismatics point to the fact that God is the same today as in the days of the New Testament. They also maintain that 1 Corinthians 13:8–13, a text often cited by cessationists to limit the time in which certain gifts function, does not limit any spiritual gift to a time period short of the Second Coming of Christ.[25]

I know that doctrinal understandings play a part in the division in the church regarding spiritual gifts, but I think that Peter Gillquist made an interesting and valid point in his book *Let's Quit Fighting About the Holy Spirit*. He wrote, "It is tragic how Satan has used to divide us the very means God gave to unite us. The Holy Spirit was given to the body of Christ to make us one."[26]

---

22. Grudem, ed., *Are Miraculous Gifts for Today?*, 11.

23. Ibid., 10.

24. Ibid.

25. Oss, "A Pentecostal/Charismatic View," 274.

26. Gillquist, *Let's Quit Fighting About the Holy Spirit*, 13.

Eschatology

Eschatology is the doctrine of last things.[27] This area of doctrine covers such topics as the rapture, the resurrection of the saints, the millennium, and the Second Coming of Christ. There is perhaps no area of doctrine about which there are more divergent views than this one. Just concerning the subject of the rapture there are at least four views, pretribulational, midtribulational, postribulational, and the partial rapture view.[28] That is, Jesus will come to take the church out of the world before the time of tribulation, part way through the time of tribulation, or after the time of tribulation that is coming upon the earth. There are also different views concerning the millennium: some Christians see it as a literal reign of Christ on the earth; others do not.[29] So there is great diversity in this area.

THE SUM OF THE MATTER

This chapter demonstrates that there are a lot of things that can divide the people of God. These obstacles have not just potentially kept people apart; they have in reality kept many apart. Some of the things that divide the church are due to spiritual problems, and some are due to doctrinal differences and practices. The different doctrinal understandings and practices are why we have so many denominations today (denominations did not exist in the New Testament church). In the next chapter, we will look at some other factors that keep different Christian churches from working together.

27. J. D. Douglas, et al, eds., *New Bible Dictionary*, s.v., "Eschatology," by R. J. Bauckham.

28. Pentecost, *Things to Come*, 156–218.

29. Erickson, *Christian Theology*, 1211.

5

Contemporary Challenges

T HE PREVIOUS TWO CHAPTERS amply illustrate that there are a lot of things that can keep the people of God apart; these things can keep Christian people from networking with each other. These obstacles need to be overcome. There are, however, a few more things that we still need to consider. These things may not be as obvious as the ones that we have looked at so far. In fact, we may not even be conscious of these dynamics being at work in our own churches. Nonetheless, these obstacles do exist, and we need to identify and remove them when we find them.

THE QUESTION

Does the church that you are a part of ever work with another Christian church or churches? You might want to break this question down further and ask, has your church ever, or does it now, work with churches of your own denomination (assuming that you are part of one) or with churches of other denominations either locally, nationally, or internationally? If the answer to this question is "no," then you might begin to ask the question "why?"

REALITY

I have been in pastoral ministry for over twenty years. Over the course of this time I have invited other churches to join us for special events (I will share the success stories later). Most of the invitations that I have sent have been to churches in my own denomination or to churches that I have some connection with (meaning that I know the pastor); however, on occasion I have invited churches and pastors with whom I did not have any prior history. My experience in all of these scenarios has been that there is generally not much support or cooperation between churches, even though all of these churches are evangelical. A few examples will illustrate what I am talking about.

One time we had Dr. Robert Cooley, then president of Gordon-Conwell Theological Seminary, speak at our church. Dr. Cooley is an archeologist, and he was going to show slides of the world of the Bible and give commentary on them. Since our church is small, we wanted to have a good crowd for him. Mailings were sent to a number of churches in the area; one of the churches that we invited was especially large. The night of the event we had thirty-three people in attendance. One woman in our congregation brought her unsaved husband, but he was the only visitor that we had that night.

One tradition that we had at our church for a number of years was that of holding a special service on Pentecost Sunday evening (what else would you expect a Pentecostal Church to do!). When we had this special service, I would invite churches from our own denomination and churches from outside of our denomination to join us for this rally. For a couple years we had some support from other churches, but for most of the years there was only one church from our own denomination that faithfully attended.

The last example that I will share took place in October of 2004. Our church helped to bring Dr. Michael Brown, an internationally known speaker, to the Boston area for a series of meetings. Two of Dr. Brown's passions are revival and Jewish evangelism. In fact, Dr. Brown has been referred to as "the foremost messianic apologist in the world."[1] As part of his time of ministry in the Boston area we were going to have a pastors' breakfast at our church. The breakfast was free, and Dr. Brown would speak.

1. Brown, *Answering Jewish Objections to Jesus*, vol. 3, back cover.

We sent mailings to about eighty churches and followed up with telephone calls. We only had a few pastors who were contacted say that they would attend, and not all of those who said they would attend actually showed up. When we saw how poor the response to our invitation was, we opened the breakfast up to our church people. That morning we only had about thirty-five people at the breakfast.

Why do these kinds of things happen? Why do churches not come together more? Why is there so little support for events that are instructional or inspirational? What is the problem? I think that the answer to these questions is multi-faceted.

Reason Number One

The local church is where we live; it is our home base. We look to it for instruction and support; it is the place where we spend most of our corporate time in the Christian faith. It is the place that we receive from. It is also a place where we give of our time, our money, and our gifts. All of this is part of being a good steward and a responsible member of Christ's body. We are "plugged in" to our local church, and we should be—every pastor wants his or her people to be committed to the local church.

Every church has its own schedule and its own ministries. There are designated times of worship, instruction, and service; some of these take place on a weekly basis. These activities require time and people in order to work. Some churches are busy on a number of nights of the week (perhaps too busy)—board meeting on Monday night, Bible study on Wednesday night, youth meeting on Saturday night, and prayer meeting on Sunday night. The upshot of all of this is that churches are sometimes too busy doing their own thing to get involved in doing something together with another church. I am not saying that this is right—only that this is part of the reason that there is not more networking among churches. People are already so busy that they cannot or will not entertain the thought of getting involved in an additional project, particularly one that is going to necessitate traveling to a place other than their own church. Time conflicts between regularly scheduled events and special events are a problem.

Reason Number Two

Dare I say it? Competition. Some churches view other churches not as comrades in the kingdom but as competition in the community; they view them as a threat. This "competition mentality" may come about because one church thinks that the distinctive doctrine of another congregation is heretical or because they want to build their own kingdom in the community. If a church views the distinctive doctrine of another congregation as heretical, they may feel that it is their mission to keep the community from the perceived error, so they seek to capture the community for themselves. The motives for aggressive evangelization of an area must be weighed. Are we really doing it to win people for the Lord or to keep them from the other church? Competition can kill unity in the body of Christ. From Jesus' prayer in John 17 it seems clear that Jesus would be opposed to such competition; he would want to dispense with it. Church leadership bears a great responsibility for this "separatist" mentality. Wherever the shepherd goes, the sheep will follow.

Reason Number Three

Fear. Churches and church leaders are afraid of one another. This may sound strange in view of the fact that all born-again people are part of the same family, but it is true. The fear exists for a number of reasons. One of the reasons was mentioned above, and that reason is doctrine. We sometimes cannot understand how people could believe differently about some things than we do. We just know that they are wrong; there must be something wrong with them to think the way they do. We had better stay away from them. There is also the fear of "sheep stealing." If a pastor or church is struggling, especially financially, they may not want to have their people join together with another church either for a special event or a continuing ministry. The reason for their fear is that they are afraid that they might lose some of their people to the other church, and they cannot afford to do that.

The challenges to unity that lie before the church seem formidable. In some ways the challenges that we face in the twenty-first century seem to be even greater than those that the New Testament church had to face. However, we should not give up or conclude that unity is an impossibility. Though the challenges are great, they are not insurmountable. The church in the first century did on occasion exemplify unity, and we can too (remember, Jesus prayed for it). We turn our attention now to examples of unity in the New Testament church.

6

Unity Is Possible:
New Testament Examples

IT IS POSSIBLE FOR the people of God to be united. The New Testament teaches this both through the examples that we find in the book of Acts and also through the practical instructions that are given in the New Testament epistles. Christians can be united within a local congregation, and they can be united between congregations. In this chapter we will look at some biblical texts that show that unity is not just an idle notion but something that can actually take place.

ACTS 1

Acts 1:14 says, "They all joined together constantly in prayer, along with the women and Mary the mother of Jesus, and with his brothers." The people referred to in this verse were the early Jewish Christians in the city of Jerusalem. Specifically, it refers to the one hundred and twenty followers of Jesus who gathered in an upper room for prayer. This group consisted of men and women, apostles and non-apostles, and members of Jesus' earthly family. They were gathered together to obey a command that Jesus had given them; he told them not to leave the city of Jerusalem but to ". . . wait for the gift my Father promised . . ." (Acts 1:4). They were to be baptized with the Holy Spirit (Acts 1:5). The unity that they demonstrated in this chapter was two-fold: it was geographic, and it was spiritual. It was geographic in that they were all physically in the same location, in an upper room in the city of Jerusalem. It was spiritual in that they were all engaged in the same activity: they were all seeking the Lord; they were praying. They were not idle as they waited for the gift that the Father promised; they actively sought the Lord. In Acts 1, we see that the church was united in obeying the words of Jesus. Their unity was in him, and it was manifest in their seeking God together in prayer.

ACTS 2

In Acts 2 we again find the church united. They were still united geographically, all being in the same place (Acts 2:1), and they were also united spiritually in that they all received the same spiritual experience: ". . . the gift my Father promised . . ." (Acts 1:4). "All of them were filled with the Holy Spirit . . ." (Acts 2:4). What they had been praying for in Acts 1 they received in Acts 2. The experience of the Spirit united them. This should not surprise us because Paul tells us in the book of Ephesians that we are to "make every effort to keep the unity of the Spirit through the bond of peace" (Eph 4:3). This text implies that there is a built-in unity that the Spirit provides.

The unity of the church can further be seen in Acts 2 in the behavior of the many people who came to believe in Jesus on the day of Pentecost. Acts 2:42 tells us that these new believers ". . . devoted themselves to the apostles' teaching and to fellowship, to the breaking of bread and to prayer." Those who joined the church that day showed unity in giving themselves to the spiritual disciplines of prayer and the apostles' teaching and participation in the community of believers in the breaking of bread and fellowship. The unity that they demonstrated was also expressed in a very tangible way: they shared their material possessions. The early believers gave to anyone as they had need (Acts 2:44–45). There was a practicality in their faith.

ACTS 4

In this chapter we find that the church was faced with a challenge; the Jewish religious leaders were putting pressure on the apostles Peter and John (and thus by extended application the rest of the church) not to speak in the name of Jesus (Acts 4:18). This was of course problematic because they knew that they were supposed to be witnesses for Jesus (Acts 1:8).

After Peter and John faced this challenge, they went back and shared the news with some of the other believers in the Jerusalem church. When the others heard the news, they, along with Peter and John, joined together in prayer and asked that God would help them to continue to speak the word in spite of the threats (Acts 4:29). Once again we find that the church was united by prayer. There was a sharing of the burden as they lifted the matter to the Lord. They supported one another spiritually. Acts 4:31 tells us that they received the answer to their prayer: ". . . they were all filled with the Holy Spirit and spoke the word of God boldly."

In this chapter we find the church united in another way as well. We are told once again that the early Christians shared materially with one another. Acts 4:32 tells us that the believers shared their possessions. Here again the church demonstrated in a practical way the unity that they had in Jesus. Their shared life included both spiritual and material sharing.

ACTS 12

In this chapter we find another example of the church in trouble, and once again the trouble came from outside of the church. This time the opposition did not come from the Jewish religious community but from the political sector. King Herod arrested some members of the church; he killed the apostle James and intended to persecute some of the other believers. The main concern of the church at this time was for one of the apostles, Peter. He had been taken into custody and placed in prison. This troubled the church because he was one of their leaders. When they became aware of the situation, they took action–they prayed. Acts 12:12 tells us that many people were gathered together at the home of Mary, the mother of John Mark, and were praying. Peter was miraculously released from prison by an angel. Once again the prayers of the church were answered, though they had a difficult time believing it when it happened (see Acts 12:14–16). Opposition and persecution have a way of bringing the people of God together.

SUMMARY OF THE ACTS PASSAGES

The examples of unity that we looked at in the book of Acts all shared one thing in common; all of the examples showed unity in a single church, the church in Jerusalem. Now I am aware that the believers in Jerusalem may have met in a number of small groups throughout the city, but the examples do concern the church in one location. The next example of unity that we will look at shows unity between congregations located in different places.

THE OFFERING FOR THE POOR IN JERUSALEM

Paul, like his Lord, was one who was very interested in bringing the people of God together. One of the ways that he sought to do this was through the collection for the poor in Jerusalem. What is significant about this particular project is that in promoting it Paul provided ". . . an active symbol of the unity of the Jewish and Gentile churches . . ."[1] The New Testament makes it clear that this was not always an easy task in the apostolic church. The Council in Jerusalem was called to settle the question of how one is saved, whether by faith in Christ alone, or faith in Christ plus other Jewish practices, especially circumcision. The decision of this council had direct bearing on Jewish and Gentile relations within the church. The decision, made with the help of the Holy Spirit (Acts 15:28), set forth the official position of the Lord of the church which called Jews and Gentiles to peace. Paul, a master "bridge builder," sought to unite the Jewish and Gentile believers

---

1. Keener, *Bible Background Commentary*, 505.

in Jesus through the practical sharing of resources. He urged those who "had" to share with those who "had not." Those who "had" in this case were the Gentile believers. Paul gave a considerable amount of time and energy to this project; this is evidenced by the number of times he wrote about this offering in the New Testament (1 Cor 16:1–4; 2 Cor 8–9). A brief look at these references will reveal that Paul received help from the churches in Achaia (Corinth), Galatia (1 Cor 16:1), and Macedonia (2 Cor 8:1–2). A quick look at a map of Paul's missionary journeys will reveal that he sought help from predominantly Gentile churches on both sides of the Mediterranean Sea. Acts 24:17 tells us that the collection for the poor in Jerusalem was delivered there.

OTHER PAULINE TEXTS

We have just seen a very practical way in which Paul worked to unite the first-century church. The gift which was delivered to Jerusalem was accepted by the Jewish people, and so there was some sense of solidarity between the Jewish and Gentile church. The fact that unity is a possibility can further be seen by some of the instructions given by Paul in the New Testament epistles. A sampling of these instructions include

> I appeal to you, brothers and sisters, in the name of our Lord Jesus Christ, that all of you agree with one another in what you say and that there be no divisions among you, but that you be perfectly united in mind and thought. (1 Corinthians 1:10)

> . . . make my joy complete by being like-minded, having the same love, being one in spirit and of one mind. (Philippians 2:2)

> May the God who gives endurance and encouragement give you a spirit of unity among yourselves as you follow Christ Jesus. (Romans 15:5 NIV)

If unity were not a possibility, then these verses do not make any sense. Why tell people to do something which is impossible?

Why hold forth some unattainable ideal? The fact that these texts do exist tells us that, with the help of God, unity is possible! It was possible for the church in the first century, and it is possible for the church now.

7

The Experience of Our Church

I BELIEVE THAT THE Lord wants each local congregation to be united within itself; each church should take seriously Paul's instruction to "make every effort to keep the unity of the Spirit through the bond of peace" (Eph 4:3). But I think that these words also have application to the larger Christian community. The apostle Paul tells us that there is "one body" (Rom 12:5; 1 Cor 12:13). The great need of the hour is for individual congregations to join hands and work together. In this chapter I would like to share with you a few things that our church has done over the years that have involved working together with other churches.

I have been pastor of a small church for twenty years; our average attendance at the time of this writing is probably about fifty people. Over the course of this time, our church has joined together with other churches on a number of occasions. Some of our collaborations have been short-term (such as a single service), and some have been more long-term. If your church is small, I think that you may have a certain edge when it comes to the issue of uniting with other churches. I am not suggesting that large churches cannot unite with other churches, not at all. What I am saying is that the smaller church may be more likely to unite with other churches. There are two main reasons for this: necessity and encouragement. The small church, because of its size, has limited people and funds. Thus, it is not able to offer the programs that a larger church can. This may cause the small church to look for others with whom they can partner in order to implement ministries that they think are needed. Encouragement can also be a motivation for unity. When a church is small, discouragement can creep in; the number of people who attend is small, and it is almost always the same faces. While the faithfulness of the saints is appreciated, sometimes people would just like to see and experience something different. Joining together with another church or churches can create a "lift" that encourages the small church. Christian unity can do much to encourage, refresh, and help the congregations that are involved. I will now share a few stories of what our small church has done.

GUTS

GUTS? That doesn't sound very Christian! Actually "GUTS" was really G.U.T.S.; it was an acronym for "Growing Under the Son." This was a youth ministry that our church participated in. The "GUTS" name was chosen because it was felt that young people would think that the name was "cool"; the name was edgy enough to grab their attention.

This ministry was born out of the mutual cooperation of some local pastors and a perceived need. The pastoral fellowship out of which the ministry was born was not an official clergy association; it was an informal group built upon relationships that the pastors had with one another. The group consisted of an American Evangelical Free pastor, a Haitian American Baptist pastor, a Korean Southern Baptist Pastor, an Indian Pentecostal pastor, and an American Pentecostal pastor whose church was predominantly Italian. The group was both ethnically and denominationally diverse. With one exception, all of the churches were located in the same city.

Our church was small; we did not have a lot of young people, and we did not have a developed youth ministry. In fact, most of the young people in our church at that time were all related to each other; they were cousins. The other pastors also had few young people in their churches. So it was decided that we would have a joint youth ministry for children. The Evangelical Free Church opened its doors to be the home base for this new work. Meetings were held weekly at the church. There were teachings and crafts in the weekly meetings. One of the enduring memories from these meetings was Pastor Shin saying, "attitude check." He would say this to the children if he felt that they were "getting off track." Workers who staffed the ministry came from the churches mentioned above. In addition to the weekly activities, there were also on occasion special outings. One time the children were taken to Pawtucket, Rhode Island, to see a Pawtucket Red Sox game (the Pawtucket Red Sox are the Triple A team for the Boston Red Sox), and one time they were taken to Kingston House/Boston Rescue Mission to serve a meal to the men there.

JOINT CONCERT OF PRAYER

Our church, which is part of a classical Pentecostal denomination, once had a joint concert of prayer with the Chinese Christian Church of New England. This event was called an International Concert of Prayer. This special service was born out of the friendship that my wife and I had with one of the pastors of the Chinese church. Our church began in the early 1970s as an ethnic Italian church and was still largely Italian at the time of the concert of prayer. At this time we also had a number of Indonesians who attended our church. The Chinese Christian Church of New England was started in 1896 by some Baptists and Congregationalists who had joined together. In time Methodists, Episcopalians, and Presbyterians also joined together with them.[1] The church is, as its name indicates, ethnically Chinese. Those who gathered at the concert of prayer were very ethnically mixed; there were Chinese, Americans, Italians, and Indonesians in attendance.

1. http://cccne.org/mission_mission.htm.

The service was held at the Chinese Christian Church of New England. We gathered that night around the following Declaration of Unity that was drafted especially for this service.

> We come together tonight as brothers and sisters. We are members of one body and believe in one true and living God. We have been purchased by the blood of Jesus Christ and are partakers of the Holy Spirit. We acknowledge "one Lord, one faith, one baptism; one God and Father of all" (Eph 4:5–6a). We, therefore, join our hands and our hearts and seek for the empowering of your church and the salvation of the world. Show us your presence and your power. Unite us in Jesus' name. Amen.

The program for the evening included this Declaration of Unity in four languages: Chinese, English, Italian, and Indonesian. During the course of the evening we worshipped using both hymns and contemporary choruses. We also prayed together; we prayed for our churches and neighborhoods, the United States, China, Indonesia, Italy, and the world. The emphasis was truly international and was in some sense a small picture of what Heaven will be. Revelation 7:9 says, "After this I looked and there before me was a great multitude that no one could count, from every nation, tribe, people and language, standing before the throne and in front of the Lamb. . . ." On another occasion the choir from the Chinese church ministered at one of our Pentecost Sunday evening rallies.

THE GREAT DEBATE

The illustration that I am going to share in this section is not exactly an example of churches working together, but I include it because it is an example of Jewish and Gentile believers in Jesus working together for a common cause (though the key organizer attended a Messianic congregation that also helped with this ministry). I think that what was accomplished was significant.

While I was a student at Gordon-Conwell Theological Seminary's Center for Urban Ministerial Education (CUME), I was working on a final paper for the Inner City Ministry course that I was taking. The topic of the paper that I was writing was how a Gentile church could reach out to a Jewish community (the community in which our church is located is over one-third Jewish). In order for me to write this paper I needed to have some understanding of Jewish thought. Around this time the parachurch ministry Jews for Jesus was re-opening their Boston branch office. Garrett Smith was the leader of the Boston branch, and I contacted him. He met with me and recommended some good resources for my paper. As a result of that meeting, he later came to speak at our church. While Garrett was at our church, he and I began to talk about Dr. Michael Brown. Dr. Brown is a Jewish believer in Jesus who has done a great deal to try to reach the Jewish people for Jesus. He is the author of a multi-volume set of books titled *Answering Jewish Objections to Jesus.*[2] Interestingly enough Dr. Brown was saved in a church that was part of the denomination that our church is affiliated with (this was significant because our denomination only has about 100 churches in the United States). Garrett said that he would like to bring Dr. Brown to the Boston area and have him debate a rabbi on a college campus. I thought that it would be nice to have him come because he was saved in one of our churches. Thus, a partnership was formed; we began to work toward the end of bringing Dr. Brown to Boston for a series of meetings, the key meeting being the debate.

I contacted Dr. Brown to see if he would be willing to come to Boston; he was, and so Garrett and I got moving on this. Our church agreed to pay for Dr. Brown's air fare, hotel, and meals. Garrett began working on setting up the debate. He contacted Rabbi Shumley Boteach, who is one of the few rabbis who will debate Dr. Brown, and he also consented to come to Boston. Garrett raised financial support for the debate from multiple sources; he also lined up a place for the debate through a chaplain that he knew in one of the major universities in Boston.

2. Brown, *Answering Jewish Objections to Jesus*, vols. 1–5.

Our church did help finance Dr. Brown's ministry in the Boston area, but I think that perhaps our most important role in this project was being the "up-front people." A lot of effort was put into advertising the debate. Ads were taken out in a number of college newspapers and a free local daily newspaper called "The Metro." When those ads were placed, I made the arrangements. The reason for this was that if the Jewish community found out that Jews for Jesus or Messianic Jews were involved in the event they probably would not attend. We made every effort to keep their name out of it.

Things progressed pretty well until about two weeks before the debate. At that time I got an email from Garrett indicating that we had big trouble. The university had caught wind of the debate and was refusing to allow it to take place on school grounds because they felt it was against the school's policy regarding proselytizing. This was a major problem. Garrett, who refused to give up, secured the Harvard Faculty Club in Boston for the debate. On October 21, 2004, the debate took place. There were over four hundred people in attendance, many of whom were from the Jewish community. As far as we know, this was the first time that an event like this was held in the Boston area. This collaborate effort resulted in a very informative evening in which, in a public debate, Jews and Christians could hear about Jesus Christ. Most importantly, it was a venue in which Jews and Gentiles could hear the scriptural evidence that Jesus is the Messiah. There was an evangelistic flavor to the evening, not a traditional evangelical altar call, but an appeal by Dr. Brown for everyone to examine the Scriptures to see if the things that he said were true. This evangelistic opportunity was made possible because Jewish and Gentiles believers in Jesus worked together.

Garrett was later asked to help arrange a similar debate in Pittsburgh, Pennsylvania. When he went to make arrangements for the debate, he told the people there that the Boston debate was possible, in part, because one church stood with them. Believers in Jesus can do more together than we can apart.

SUMMARY

The few experiences that I have shared in this chapter illustrate that believers of different denominations and ethnicities can work together for kingdom purposes. The groups involved do not have to be large in order to be effective or have a significant impact. What is necessary is the sharing of a vision and the willingness to work together. If these things are present, there is no telling what can be accomplished; finances, if necessary, will come along the way. The examples shared in this chapter show some of the ministries that believers can partner in: youth ministry, prayer, and evangelism. I am sure that there are other ministries in which believers can partner as well. These examples simply demonstrate that there is a potential in working together. If there is a kingdom need that your church has not been able to fill, then joining together in partnership with believers from another church or churches may be what is necessary in order to get the need met. These examples illustrate how important relationships in the body of Christ are. All of these ministries came into being because of relationships that the leaders had with one another. The leaders, in turn, were able to encourage the people in their churches or groups to work with believers from other ministries. As a result, things that may not have happened otherwise took place.

8

In the Deep

IN HIS BOOK, *Can You See God in This Picture?* John King makes reference to a meeting called "In the Deep" that is held at a Pentecostal church.[1] The "In the Deep" meetings were held in our church. I wish I could say that I came up with the idea for this ministry, but that is not so. This ministry did not come about as the result of a decision made by the leadership of our church; it came into being through the friendship and initiative of a number of young adults who were musically gifted and desired to serve the Lord through music. They became the worship team for the ministry known as "In the Deep." These young people presented the idea for the ministry to the church board and asked if they could have the services at our church. The board approved their request.

THE TEAM

The makeup of the worship team for "In the Deep" is as interesting as the ministry itself. With one exception, all of the members of the group are in their twenties; both men and women are in the worship team. When the ministry began, the members of the group came from a number of local churches representing different denominations (a couple of the worship team members have since married into our church, and I mean that quite literally).

1. King, *Can You See God in This Picture?*, 133.

Members of the team have included representatives from Baptist, Christian and Missionary Alliance, non-denominational, and Pentecostal church backgrounds. The instruments that are used in worship are the acoustic guitar, electric guitar, bass guitar, electronic keyboard, piano, and drums. A number of the musicians in the group can play multiple instruments, so they are able to use different instruments for different musical arrangements. There is one member of the leadership team who does not play or sing in the group; she helps with communications and refreshments.

THE SETTING

"In the Deep" is held in the sanctuary of our church on Saturday evenings at 7 P.M. I am not exactly sure why they chose this time. Having it on Saturday night probably keeps it from conflicting with most local church services (which I am sure the pastors appreciate). Meeting on a weekend probably also makes it easier for people to attend when they are less busy with work and school responsibilities.

When people enter the sanctuary, there is usually pre-recorded music playing. The lights in the sanctuary are kept low; sometimes candles are lit in the window bays. There are blinds on the windows so that even during months when it is still light at 7 P.M., light can be kept to a minimum in the sanctuary. This is done so that people will feel more comfortable; they will be able to worship without feeling that they are being watched by others, and they will not be distracted by others. People are free to raise their hands, clap their hands, bow their heads, or kneel. They can stand or sit, and they are free to worship as loudly or as softly as they wish; they can be either demonstrative or reserved as they express their worship. There is no prescribed norm that they must conform to. The meeting is very informal, people who attend come dressed casually, and wearing jeans is okay.

THE MINISTRY

The slogan for "In the Deep" is "ageless, passionate worship"; the service is not a concert—those who attend are not to just sit back and listen. They are expected to be participants, not spectators. "In the Deep" is advertised as a worship service, and that is what it is. For one hour God is the focus of the meeting. There is no sermon and no offering; worship takes the place of prominence. The worship music that the team plays is for the most part contemporary Christian music. The music used includes songs by the David Crowder Band, Chris Tomlin, Hillsong, Matt Redman, Charlie Hall, and sometimes an old hymn of the church like "Be Thou My Vision" is sung. The group also on occasion does some original material. During the course of the evening Scripture verses are read, and there is a quiet time for people to close themselves in with the Lord and pray. At the end of the hour when the worship time is closing people are invited to come to the front of the sanctuary if they would like to be prayed for. A couple of members of the worship team are available to pray for those who respond to this invitation.

After the service light refreshments are served in the lower auditorium. There are soft drinks, fruit, chips, cookies, and other light refreshments that people may partake of. During this time people get to talk with one another and meet new friends. The young people sometimes refer to this time of fellowship as "hanging out." They spend time together. I have even heard that after this time of "hanging out" some of them will go out for ice cream at a small restaurant located just down the street from the church.

HOW "IN THE DEEP" IS ADVERTISED

How do people come to know about "In the Deep"? Well, interestingly enough, there is not a lot of formal advertising that is done. No ads are run in local newspapers, and there are no commercials on the radio. The event is advertised electronically and by word of mouth. People who attend "In the Deep" can put their e-mail address on a list to be notified of future services. In addition to this, the leaders use Facebook to advertise the meetings. Most of those who attend do so because of the personal relationships that they have with members of the worship team or others who attend. Word of mouth plays a significant part in making the event known; friends tell friends. One member of the worship team told me that pastors' wives and people from churches that no one in the worship team knows have shown up at "In the Deep" services. This ministry is a good example of what it means to network.

WHAT IS THE ATTRACTION?

Why do people attend "In the Deep"? Saturday evening is typically a night that most people, especially young people, reserve for activities like bowling, going to the movies, or partying. I posed the "why" question to members of the worship team, and they told me that some people may attend because they like the music, but they think there are two main reasons why people are attracted to the services. The first is a desire to worship, to relate to God, the other is a desire to be with friends. The services provide for fellowship with God and with one another (1 John 1:3). The Bible places a high priority on these two things; one could list many verses which deal with cultivating these two kinds of fellowship. In his book, *Love, Acceptance, and Forgiveness: Being Christian in a Non-Christian World*, Jerry Cook identifies worship and fellowship as two things that help produce Spirit-filled Christians.[2] One of the members of the worship team said that he felt that the "In the Deep" service was a place to pour out and to be poured into, a place to rejoice and a place to feel the weight of conviction. In these services young people have the opportunity to meet with God directly and through their brothers and sisters in Christ.

---

2. Cook with Baldwin, *Love, Acceptance, and Forgiveness*, 49.

A PROPHETIC SIGN

As I sat in one "In the Deep" service, a passage was read from Acts 4. The text that was read reported how the early church prayed together after Peter and John had been threatened by the Sanhedrin (Acts 4:23–31). It occurred to me after hearing that passage of Scripture read that prayer and worship are two things that can bring the people of God together. Part of the reason for this is that, for the most part, we do not let doctrinal distinctives get in the way here. When it comes to prayer and worship, the secondary distinctives that often divide us do not seem so important. When we worship and pray, we are not really worried about whether the person to our right or left is a Calvinist or Arminian in their theology or whether their church baptizes infants or only adults. Those issues fall by the wayside. One of the members of the worship team told me that he sees "In the Deep" as a ministry that can break down denominational walls. By this he did not mean the destroying of denominations but rather the downplaying or removal of the labels that sometimes divide Christians. When people attend "In the Deep," they take off their labels; as they gather they are not Baptists, Pentecostals, or any other denomination; they are brothers and sisters in Christ, members of one body.

While the "In the Deep" services are not the only place that Christians of different denominations are coming together (there have been, and certainly will be others), I believe that it is one prophetic sign of what is coming. I believe that God is beginning to move upon the church to get together to work together, not in the sense of erasing denominations but in the sense of partnering with one another. I believe that the prayer Jesus prayed in John 17 is beginning to be noticeably answered and that it will be answered in even greater measure in the days to come. It seems logical to believe this as the time of the Lord's return draws nearer.

9

International Networking

I BELIEVE THAT THERE are signs of the coming together of God's people in many places. In the previous two chapters I have given you some examples of how our church has participated in, or been impacted by, expressions of Christian unity. In this chapter, I will share some additional evidence that God is working to bring his people, the church, together. The examples that I will share in this chapter come from my personal knowledge of the events or persons involved. I hope that you will see the hand of God at work in these examples that I will share.

MY WIFE AND I

My wife, Cindy, and I have been overseas a number of times. We have both been to Indonesia twice. On the first trip she and I both preached at a church in Solo on the island of Java. Also during this trip I taught at a Bible school in Surabaya, and a Charismatic seminary at Jokjakarta. Our second trip to Indonesia was of a more social nature; we went there to attend the weddings of some friends who used to attend our church in Massachusetts. While I did not do any preaching or teaching on this trip, I did participate in the church services for both of these weddings. My wife and I have also both been to Africa. However, the African trips have been different. While we have both been to the continent of Africa, we have not traveled to the same countries. I went to Zimbabwe in 2006 and again in 2008 with Barnabas Ministries.

My wife went to Kenya in 2007 with Matthew 28 Ministries. Both of these ministries are missions organizations. These trips to Africa in particular showed signs of Christian unity.

In 2006 when I went to Zimbabwe the team that I was part of conducted pastors' seminars in the city of Harare (the capital of Zimbabwe), and in a couple of other cities. Barnabas Ministries, which was founded by Drs. David and Jeanne Wynns, serves mostly the countries of Africa. The ministers that they send out are, for the most part, from various classical Pentecostal denominations including the Assemblies of God, the International Church of the Foursquare Gospel, and the International Fellowship of Christian Assemblies. Many of the people who attend the pastors' conferences are also Pentecostals. However, in Zimbabwe, these Pentecostals are from denominations native to their land, groups like the Apostolic Faith Mission and the Pentecostal Assemblies of Zimbabwe, rather than from the denominations of the speakers sent out by Barnabas Ministries. At one conference that I ministered at, due to the makeup of the group who attended, it was felt that, in addition to English, which is the national language, the sessions should also be translated into the native language of Shona. We had at least two interpreters for this conference; one of them was a Presbyterian minister, complete with his collar. He helped to make plain to the people what the ministers from the United States were saying.

In 2007, my wife went to Kenya with Matthew 28 Ministries, a ministry founded by Dr. Jewel Hyun. On this trip she was part of a team with three other women; all of the other women on the trip were of Asian descent. The group was also denominationally mixed. The mission of Matthew 28 Ministries was to teach African pastors/leaders about the subject of the biblical equality—that Christian men and women are equal and can serve together in ministry. The teaching sessions were taught by two of the women from Matthew 28 Ministries and some men who were national pastors. One of the pastors was a Baptist and one was a Pentecostal. The seminars were attended by men and women alike from a number of different denominations.

AFRICAN LIBRARY

This is another example of Christian unity that has to do with Africa. When I went to Zimbabwe in 2006, I taught some classes at Living Waters Theological Seminary in Harare. The school is affiliated with the Apostolic Faith Mission. The Apostolic Faith Mission is a Trinitarian Pentecostal group. The principal of this school, Dr. Constantine Murefu, was a classmate of mine at Zion Bible Institute. While I was at Living Waters, I asked if I could see the library. The dean of the school took me to see it. He told me that they did not have a lot of newer books. As I looked at the shelves, I could see that some of the books, especially the Bible commentaries, were very old and worn; they also had a lot of paperback books. I asked the dean if they would accept donations of books for the library. He told me that they would.

When I got back to the United States, I told our church that I would like to start an African Book Fund. The church got behind it, and we began to collect money for books. I contacted some Christian authors and publishers to see if they might be able to donate some books for the project or offer them to us at a discount since we were sending them overseas. The results of these inquires was very encouraging. We had some books given to us and some sold to us at substantial discounts. One donation that we received from a Christian publisher was pretty overwhelming; they sent us seventy-seven books (many of them hardcover) for free! I would estimate that we have sent about 200 books to the Living Waters library. We have also on one occasion helped the school with some finances. While our church and Living Waters Theological Seminary are both Pentecostal, they are part of two different denominations, so this is in some small way a demonstration of Christian unity.

INDONESIAN LIBRARY

The story I am going to share here is somewhat similar to the one I shared about the African library. However, this project predates the African Book Project. Hanny Setiawan, a native Indonesian, attended our church for about seven years. He is the son of a pastor on the island of Java; he was in the United States for schooling. At one point he approached me with the idea of building a two thousand volume theological reference library in Indonesia. I liked the idea and presented it to the church. The church was in favor of it, and we began to collect money for books. We called this venture "The Indonesian Book Project." The motto that we drafted for it was "Create a Library, Cultivate a Leader."

For this project we also received donations of books from authors and discounts from publishers. In fact, the same publisher who sent us seventy-seven free books for Zimbabwe also sent us seventy-seven free books for Indonesia. So far we have purchased about two hundred books for Indonesia, and there are more funds available to purchase additional books. We are now in the process of shipping the books that we have. Our church and the church that we are working with in Indonesia are both Pentecostal, but we are part of different denominational groups. So here again is another small sign of the coming together of the people of God.

These two book projects represent a redistribution of wealth. We, in the American church, who have more ample resources, are seeking to help supply our sisters and brothers in other countries with resources that they cannot afford to purchase for themselves at this time. These projects are also both educational in nature and have the potential to yield multiplied returns. Those who use the resources will learn, and they can pass on their knowledge to others, who may in turn also teach additional people.

THE HOUSE OF PRISCA AND AQUILA

In the New Testament Prisca and Aquila were a husband and wife team who hosted house churches and shared together in ministry

(Acts 18:26; 1 Cor 16:19). The House of Prisca and Aquila (www.houseofpriscaandaquila.com) is the publishing label started by Drs. William and Aída Spencer; the Spencers are both professors at Gordon-Conwell Theological Seminary. Dr. Aída Spencer is a professor of New Testament, and Dr. William Spencer is a theology professor. The stated purpose of this publishing label is ". . . to produce quality books that expound accurately the word of God to empower women and men to minister together in a multicultural church." The Spencers have a number of people who work with them in the House of Prisca and Aquila. These people come from a number of different races and Christian denominations. There are people on the team from Baptist, Presbyterian, Methodist, Conservative Congregational, Pentecostal, Advent Christian, and African Methodist Episcopal churches. While they most certainly would have differences of opinion regarding some points of doctrine, they are all committed to the Bible as the word of God and the stated purposes of the publishing label. This ministry is international in that two of the titles already published by the House of Prisca and Aquila have contributors from around the world. Writers who have contributed to House of Prisca and Aquila books have come from countries such as Kenya, Zimbabwe, South Africa, Congo, Germany, and India to name a few. This publishing label is living proof that born-again believers from different church traditions can work together for God's kingdom (and they are in some measure doing it globally).

IMPACTING THE WORLD

The word *international* can be a little overwhelming; it sounds so big. However, this chapter shows that it is possible to impact the world. In order to do this, you do not need to have a lot of money or a large staff; in fact, in some situations you do not even need to leave your home country. Consider the possibilities!

10

Around the World

IN CHAPTER 8, I said that the "In the Deep" worship service is one prophetic sign of what God is doing in the world today: the Lord is bringing believers together. In chapters 7 and 9 I gave you examples of Christians working together, across denominational lines in children's ministry, evangelism, and education. All of the examples that I have given up to this point have involved believers in the United States. In some cases we have seen Christians in the United States working together with each other, and in other cases we have seen Christians in the United States partnering with believers in other countries. What about the rest of the world? Is this same move toward unity taking place in other countries? Are believers in other countries also joining hands to work together for kingdom purposes?

In order to answer this question, I have asked people in different parts of the world to let me know about movements toward unity that they are aware of. These friends and acquaintances have served as my eyes and ears on foreign soil. In calling on these individuals, I have sought to get a "grass roots," rather than academic, look at what is going on in these countries. So most of the material presented here did not come from books or Web sites but from people who have firsthand knowledge of the field. I appreciate very much their willingness to share what is taking place in their countries. I believe that their contributions will confirm the fact that God is doing a great work in bringing believers together in our day. There are signs that the prayer of Jesus is being answered in greater measure.

A friend of mine, who lives in Australia, told me that in his country Christians from various churches work together. However, in many cases they do so through parachurch organizations such as Scripture Union Australia, Prison Fellowship Australia, and Youth for Christ. The same holds true in the United States. Parachurch organizations like Young Life and Youth With A Mission (YWAM) bring believers from various church traditions together to work for common Christian causes such as evangelism.

While parachurch organizations are helpful in bringing believers together, I want to focus attention primarily on churches that decide to work together without any "outside help." In other words, the churches themselves decided that they would work together. I think this is highly significant. In the following accounts you will read of churches working together or churches forming collaboratives in which they can work together for common causes. The information that you will find below is not equally balanced throughout the world. For example, I have no information from South America but quite a bit from Africa and the Far East. I apologize for this imbalance, but I had to work with the contacts that I had. I could have done some library research to fill in the gaps but preferred to have this be more of a grassroots report than an academic one. In spite of the limitations of the reports, I believe that they serve to illustrate the point that the Lord is uniting the church in different parts of the world today. We turn our attention now to what is happening in other parts of the globe.

SINGAPORE

Pastor Daniel Chua of City Church supplied me with some information about alliances and networks in the church in Singapore. One of the partnerships that has emerged is called Ignite Alliance. This ministry was birthed out of the relationships among the leaders of the churches in Singapore who shared a common vision. Ignite Alliance's Facebook page says that they exist to help take up the cause of transforming campuses, the world, and themselves through prayer and proclamation. The ministry is especially concerned with reaching young people between the ages of four and fourteen. They believe that this is one of the keys to national revival. Ignite Alliance hosts an annual youth conference that draws people from about forty to fifty different churches. In addition to the youth conference, they host a monthly prayer breakfast to gather leaders together to foster revival through prayer and friendship.

Ignite Alliance is also a part of the National Prayer Alliance under the leadership of Rev. Edmund Chan. This alliance gathers key prayer leaders from many denominations once a month to pray. In addition, Ignite Alliance is also a part of Youth More Than Gold. This was an initiative to mobilize Christians to serve at the Youth Olympic Games that were held in Singapore in 2010. As of this writing, this initiative was being supported by other Christian ministries including: the Evangelical Fellowship of Singapore, Singapore Campus Crusade for Christ, the Bible Society of Singapore, and Youth With A Mission. The brochure for Youth More Than Gold states that they aim to

- Initiate an outreach campaign to engage youth and the nation.
- Involve the Church to come together and bless the community through hospitality and service.
- Inspire the next generation to live beyond the finished line.[1]

What is interesting about this particular movement, though it is not the main focus of this book, is that parachurch organizations banded together for a common cause. The Youth More Than

---

1. This brochure can be found on the Youth More Than Gold Web site (www.ymtg.sg), accessed October 2009.

Gold brochure also asked churches to consider being hosts for some of the events that were planned.[2]

In addition to these networks, Pastor Chua reports that in Singapore they have an annual retreat in January for prayer and friendship. At the most recent retreat, they had about 500 pastors from around 80 churches attend. Pastor Chua said that one of the reasons Christians in Singapore work together is because they believe that the Lord wants believers to be one.

INDIA

Dr. Finny Philip, principal of Filadelfia Bible College in Udaipur, India, has told me that churches in Northern India also come together in unity. In this book I have focused on the subject of spiritual unity; that is, I have talked about Bible-believing Christians, who hold to certain fundamental evangelical truths, linking arms to work together on biblical ministries. I am sure that this dynamic is at work in India. However, the report that Dr. Philip provided me with describes cooperation among the churches of Northern India that may be somewhat surprising to believers in the West. In Northern India, churches from a wide range of denominational backgrounds join together in cooperation; the church groups that join together include Pentecostal, Anglican, Catholic, and Orthodox churches. This type of cooperation is largely unheard of in the West.

One of the things that helps foster cooperation among these different Christian denominations is a group known as Udaipur Christian Fellowship (UCF) in Udaipur, Rajasthan. This group exists for the purpose of promoting unity and partnership between the churches. The members of this fellowship include Catholic, Orthodox, Protestant (Anglicans), Pentecostals, and members of other independent groups as well. This fellowship provides a platform or base which causes the churches to work together.

Another thing that contributes to the cooperation of the various Christian denominations in Northern India is persecu-

2. Ibid.

tion. When radical Hindus bring opposition against Christians, the churches work together to make presentations to the government; the churches present a united front. In spite of their doctrinal differences, the churches realize that if one group suffers all could potentially suffer because all are recognized as being part of the Christian faith.

In Northern India they also have what they call Unity Week; this is held each year in the month of January. During the course of Unity Week, there are programs that are held in various churches that include times of worship and listening to the Scriptures being preached. There is a good deal of pulpit exchange that goes on during this time. For example, a Catholic or Orthodox priest may preach in a Pentecostal church, and a worship leader from a Pentecostal church might lead worship in a more liturgical church. During the Christmas season, the Indian churches also have joint carol services in which people from different churches join together; they also pray for the nation during this time. The partnership of Christian churches working together on spiritual and political issues has helped put a lot of the disunity between churches to rest.

KENYA

Pastor Sammy Nyaranga, a Baptist minister in Kenya, has told me that the churches in Kenya work together across denominational lines in a number of different ministries. Two of the main reasons why they work together are to obey Scripture and to meet various human needs. The ministries in which they cooperate address both the spiritual and physical needs of the country.

One of the great problems on the continent of Africa is the problem of HIV/AIDS. This pandemic leaves many orphans in its wake. Pastor Sammy's church has an orphanage for thirty-five children. They take in children who come from various church backgrounds—Catholic, Pentecostal, Salvation Army, Anglican, and other church groups—because people from all of these groups are affected by the AIDS problem. They welcome the help of other churches in this ministry, whether it be visiting the children or helping provide food for them.

Another social ministry that they collaborate on is that of helping displaced persons. After the elections in 2007, there was an outbreak of violence in Kenya (my wife had been there just prior to these outbreaks). This violence resulted in some people's homes being burned; with no place to call home, many people were displaced. The churches in Kenya sought to help the displaced by praying for them, counseling them, and providing them with food, tents, and blankets. Churches of various denominations participated in this effort to help the suffering.

The violence that erupted after the elections in 2007 was frequently the result of tribal tensions, one tribe attacking another. The churches of Kenya have sought to bring tribal reconciliation to the people; churches that have participated in these efforts have come from a number of tribes and denominations. Reconciliation is clearly a matter very near to the heart of God (Matt 18:15–20; Eph 2:14–18).

The churches in the Nairobi area also hold joint prayer meetings, worship services, and evangelistic services. There is also a national day of prayer that brings together all of the churches of Kenya; governmental leaders join in this gathering. This gathering is to pray for the nation. Combined evangelistic services are organized by a fellowship of pastors from various denominations.

One last area that I will mention is that of education. The churches in Kenya work together to train and equip leaders. This training is Bible based and is given to pastors to help them be more effective leaders in their churches. This brief report shows us that the church in Kenya is partnering in many different ministries to help meet the needs of the nation.

SOUTH AFRICA

Rev. Nancy Hudson is a Pentecostal minister who is ordained with the International Fellowship of Christian Assemblies (IFCA). She is a missionary to South Africa and oversees the Christian

Assemblies of South Africa (CASA). In our correspondence she has shared with me a number of instances of mutual cooperation among the Christians of South Africa. For example, she made a trip to Mozambique with some of the pastors in her network. This trip was arranged by a man from the Methodist Church who asked them to participate. People from a local Charismatic Church and from the Methodist Church were also a part of this trip. The group did evangelism in Mozambique, showing the *Jesus* film to the people there.[3] There was tremendous response to the film. In fact, the pastor of the Methodist Church has asked Rev. Hudson for help in following up with the new converts in Mozambique. She has some pastors who can speak the Shangaan language, which is spoken in Mozambique. The Methodist pastor has asked that these pastors help disciple the new converts in Mozambique and help raise up church leadership there. Rev. Hudson also told me that her church has had fellowship with and done outreach with the Lutheran Church in South Africa. Some of the Lutheran young people even participate in the youth group of the Pentecostal Church. The Lutheran Church has also contributed clothing for Rev. Hudson to take to the poor in Malawi. The people from her Pentecostal church have attended conferences hosted by the Anglican Church. On a number of occasions Rev. Hudson has spoken to ladies groups in both the Lutheran and Anglican churches. Lastly, Rev. Hudson has preschools at each of her churches that are attended by children from a number of church backgrounds including Catholic and Lutheran churches. There is significant cooperation among Christian churches in the area where Rev. Hudson ministers.

Jackie Thomas, who is originally from Barbados, attended our church when she was visiting in the United States; she currently serves in South Africa with the missions organization Operation Mobilization. She, with the help of Martin De Lange (who is also

---

3. *The Jesus Film*, Campus Crusade for Christ International, 2003 (25th anniversary edition).

with Operation Mobilization), provided me with a couple of other examples of Christian unity in the country of South Africa.

In an area known as Witbank, a couple of Dutch Reformed Churches have teamed up with Charismatic and Pentecostal churches to minister to the community. The Pentecostal Church that is involved is part of the Apostolic Faith Mission, a Trinitarian Pentecostal group. These churches partner in prayer and in outreach to the community.

In Pretoria, there is something called "Moot for Jesus" (Moot is a geographic area). This, like the ministry in Witbank, is a joint effort between the Dutch Reformed Church and Pentecostal churches (again the AFM church). This group takes a stand against crime in the community and does outreaches including open-air meetings. The ministers of these two church groups also participate in pulpit exchanges. These joint efforts are a good testimony to the unbelieving world and help the churches to be more effective as they labor together rather than apart.

UGANDA

The country of Uganda has suffered in many ways. A lot of this suffering has directly affected the children of the land. Some children have been abducted and forced to become child soldiers, and others have been orphaned due to war or the AIDS epidemic.[4] I first became aware of the situation in Uganda through a number of different sources: a video in the Transformation Video series;[5] hearing the testimony of Grace Akallo, a former child soldier in Uganda who spoke at a church in our area; and from the Ugandans who have attended our church. The problems affecting the children in Uganda are significant, and the church has been active in seeking to address the needs of these children.

One church that is taking great steps to address the needs of children is Kampala Pentecostal Church, which is now called

4. www.watoto.com.

5. *An Unconventional War*, Global Net Productions, The Sentinel Group, 2006.

Watoto Church.[6] I first became aware of this church from a Ugandan woman who attended our church. Her home church was the Kampala Pentecostal Church. This church is very intentional about caring for orphans. Their motto is "Rescue a Child, Raise a Leader, Restore a Nation."[7] The remainder of the information found in this paragraph can be found on their Web site.[8] The church has created a model for taking care of orphans; they take eight orphans, or at-risk children, and place them in a home. This home has a mother who cares for them. In essence, the church creates a family for the children. In this home the children are provided with food and shelter; their health, educational, and spiritual needs are addressed as well. These homes are not traditional orphanages. The church has presented this model to other churches so that they too can care for children in a way that has proven to be effective. Their hope is that 10,000 churches will adopt the Watoto model and be able to rescue more than two million children in need. The church is thus seeking to partner with the larger Christian community by sharing their knowledge so that the needs of the children throughout Africa can be more effectively met.

I have seen firsthand some of the effects of the work that the Watoto Church is doing. In 2008 I had the privilege of hearing and seeing the Watoto Children's Choir minister in a neighboring city. The choir is made up of some of the children to whom the church ministers. One cannot help but be struck by the dignity, joy, and confidence that is evident in the lives of these young people. The brokenness that these children have experienced is being replaced with the vision of a life with a hope and a future (Jer 29:11). At the concert people were given the opportunity to sponsor a child (one can also sponsor a child through the Watoto Web site). In making this opportunity available, the church is

6. http://en.wikipedia.org/wiki/Watoto_Church.

7. www.watoto.com.

8. Ibid.

networking with the wider Christian world to help make a differ-ence in the lives of Uganda's children.

Watoto Church also started cell groups, small fellowship groups, to care for the people who attend their church. This model also proved to be effective, and they shared their model with All Saints Church (Anglican). The Anglican Church also adopted the cell group format when they saw how effective it was. Here again we see a willingness to share, to help the larger body of Christ. While these churches may not be physically join-ing together, they are partnering to help meet the spiritual and physical needs of the people in Uganda.

ZIMBABWE

Dr. Constantine Murefu, who was a classmate of mine at Zion Bible Institute (now Zion Bible College), is currently principal of Living Waters Theological Seminary in Harare, Zimbabwe. He has informed me that the church in Zimbabwe is coming togeth-er around a number of important spiritual issues. Churches are joining together to pray, evangelize, disciple, and do visitation.

In addition to the more traditional spiritual emphases of the church, the churches in Zimbabwe are also coming together to address political and national concerns. For example, in 2006 because of the severe inflation and political turmoil in the coun-try, the Apostolic Faith Mission, one of the oldest and largest Pentecostal denominations in Zimbabwe, the Roman Catholic bishops, and churches from Baptist, Methodist, and other Protestant denominations came together to pray for Zimbabwe. Those gathered at this meeting prayed for God to heal their land. Various political leaders were invited to participate in this prayer effort. The President of Zimbabwe was in attendance and offered both a speech and prayer for the country. The church is rising up to tell politicians the kind of Zimbabwe that they want.

The situation that Dr. Murefu has described sounds in some ways similar to what Dr. Finny Philip reported about what the churches in Northern India are doing in their country. Churches are working for both the spiritual and social renewal of the country. The partnerships in Zimbabwe are fostered through three main umbrella organizations: the Evangelical Fellowship of Zimbabwe (EFZ,) which represents 240 denominations; the Zimbabwe Council of Churches (ZCC); and the Zimbabwe Council of Catholic Bishops Conference (ZCCBC). The Apostolic Faith Mission is a member of both the Evangelical Fellowship of Zimbabwe (EFZ) and the Zimbabwe Council of Churches (ZCC). Dr. Murefu has told me that there has been an ecumenical movement in the country since 2006.

WORLD REPORT

The accounts that you have just read are by no means exhaustive, but they are important. A brief survey of these reports from around the world indicates that churches in a number of different places are partnering together in biblical ministries. They are addressing the social needs in their lands, taking care of orphans (Jas 1:27) ,and meeting some of the other human needs that Jesus spoke about in Matthew 25—things such as feeding the hungry and clothing those in need of clothes.

Churches in the global community are also giving themselves to partnering in the traditional spiritual practices of the church, things like prayer, worship, evangelistic outreach, and discipleship. These are all clearly biblical priorities (Acts 2:42; 4:23–31; 12:5; 13:1–2; Matt 28:18–20; Mark 16:15). The global church is in some places also coming together in less traditional ways to address the government concerning matters of policy and justice. It looks as if God is at work to answer the prayer of Jesus in John 17.

11

Partnership Possibilities

THERE ARE MANY POSSIBILITIES for networking in the body of Christ. These possibilities basically fall into two categories: the kinds of partnerships that churches can enter into, and the types of ministries that churches can partner in. In this chapter I will give you a brief overview of both the types of relationships that churches can enter into and the ministries that they can most easily share together in. This survey will by no means be exhaustive but merely representative of some of the various ways that the church of Jesus Christ can be connected. Perhaps this chapter will help spark your imagination regarding some other partnerships that are available to you that are not listed here.

PARTNERSHIPS

Connections between churches vary; some of the connections are more formal or structured and others are less formal. Some associations are entered into voluntarily, while others may be more set due to things like denominational affiliation. It should be noted here that partnerships can potentially be either long-term or short-term. There are some partnerships that are only for a season, to meet a specific need or crisis, while others are of a more enduring nature.

International Missions Partnerships

Jesus said that the gospel will be preached in the whole world (Matt 24:14). He thus gave a charge, or commission, to the church to go into all the world and make disciples (Matt 28:19). In view of this, many churches, especially those that are affiliated with a denomination, participate in international missions. The denomination either has, or seeks to establish, ministries in other parts of the world. These ministries may include the planting of churches or the building of schools or orphanages. Many congregations that participate in international missions do so in the form of financial giving; the local church collects funds and directs them, through proper channels, to the works elsewhere in the world. These funds may be collected monthly, quarterly, or in response to a special appeal. Financial partnerships are probably the most common form of involvement that many churches have with international missions.

In the International Fellowship of Christian Assemblies (IFCA), the denomination that I am a part of, there is an additional form of involvement that one can pursue. The IFCA has a program that is known as World Impact Teams; this is a short-term missions program. In this program a person can apply to go to the mission field. A typical World Impact Teams trip lasts between ten days and two weeks. While this is a short period of time, it does supply a person with the opportunity to do more than give financially to the cause of missions; it allows a person to actually do some hands-on missions work. I am sure that there are other denominations with similar programs. Time spent on the mission field will do more to change a believer than putting an offering in an envelope ever will. I speak from experience regarding this. Some Christians may actually receive their call to missions through a program like World Impact Teams.

The two forms of participation that I have just mentioned are very traditional in that they are done within the framework of a denomination or church network. These should not, however, be thought to be the only international partnerships that churches can enter into. There are other options open as well.

In chapter 9, I shared briefly about our church's African Book Project. This is one example of a "different" kind of partnership. This ministry of our church has helped build up the library of a seminary in Harare, Zimbabwe. The school that we are helping is not affiliated with our denomination. The partnership that connected our church with the seminary is very informal; it was established not on the basis of denominational affiliation but on the basis of friendship. It is a relational connection. As I mentioned earlier, the current principal of the school and I were classmates in Bible school. The school did not solicit our help for their library. I offered to help, and shortly afterward our church also began to give to help this school.

National Missions Partnerships

In addition to international missions, there is another type of missions that churches can partner in. This other type of missions is home missions. Home missions are an effort on the part of a denomination or, in some cases, a local church to plant additional congregations in the country where the church or denomination is based. Denominations typically seek to plant churches in areas that do not have one of their churches. I suspect that the most common form of local church involvement in national missions is also financial giving. Funds are collected and deployed to the new church plant.

Home missions programs also, in certain situations, provide an additional opportunity for more personal involvement for some believers. For example, one way in which new churches are planted is by taking a group of people from an existing church and sending them off with a church-planting pastor to help start a new work. These people serve as a base, or core, for the new church. Using this approach is of benefit to the church-planting pastor in that he or she does not start without any people. I am sure this is an encouragement to the pastor. This method of church planting also provides the new church with workers as well as some local financial support for itself.

Local Church Partnerships

This next type of partnership that I would like to speak about is local church partnerships. Unlike home missions partnerships that may involve a church in New York helping to fund a church in Arizona, local church partnerships take place within a more confined geographic area, such as a city, town, or county. These partnerships can take a couple of different forms.

One form that these partnerships can take is that of an urban-suburban partnership. In this partnership a church in the city and one in a suburban area decide to work together. There is a book entitled *Linking Arms, Linking Lives* devoted to discussing this very subject. It gives specific examples of churches that have partnered in this way; it also shows how both urban and suburban churches can benefit from this type of partnership.[1] This form of partnership may likely, but not always, involve churches from the same denomination.

Another kind of local partnership that can be established is one in which churches in a particular city, or in neighboring areas, decide to work together. I am thinking here specifically of partnerships between churches from different denominations. This particular model is perhaps more difficult to get started, but it is not impossible. It could potentially come about through a local clergy association, the personal friendships of some local pastors, or a need which impacts the community as a whole. There may be exceptions to this, but I think that in the majority of cases if churches are going to partner together, pastors/leaders have to be involved in order for this kind of partnership to get started and continue. As I mentioned in chapter 7, our church worked together with churches of other denominations in the

---

1. Sider, et al., *Linking Arms, Linking Lives.*

youth ministry, G.U.T.S. This ministry began because of the relationships of the pastors of the various churches.

THE MINISTRIES

In the first part of this chapter, I gave you an idea of some of the ministry connections that might be made by churches. Having now seen some of the different kinds of partnerships that may be established, let us now move on to consider the "what" of the partnerships. What types of ministries might churches join together in? I believe that there are three ministries in which churches can quite easily work together, three in which the church can show unity to an unbelieving world. These areas are prayer, evangelism, and ministries of mercy. These are all biblical ministries and ones in which our differences of practice and doctrine should not be significant obstacles to working together.

Prayer

Prayer is a very foundational practice in the Christian faith, regardless of one's denomination. All followers of Jesus are to pray. The New Testament is replete with both admonitions to pray (Luke 18:1; Eph 6:18; 1 Tim 2:1–2; 1 Thess 5:17) and examples of prayer (Acts 1:14; 4:23–31; 12:5, 12; 13:3; 16:25). In addition to the biblical witness concerning prayer, we are aware of prayer's importance because of our life experiences. There are many things in our lives that we cannot change, and we need the Lord to intervene on our behalf. In its simplest form, prayer is communication with God. All Christians believe in the same God, the God of the Bible. This is a good starting point. With this common rallying point, Christians should be able to get together to seek the Lord. It is true that we have our differences about prayer, such as the posture that we should assume in prayer (sit, stand, kneel, hands clasped, hands raised, etc.). However, Christians should be able to put these differences aside for the greater good of entreating the Lord to be gracious to us and to others. In the Bible people from different places prayed together (Acts14:23; 20:36). The same can happen today. Concerts of prayer are one contemporary example of believers from different places (churches) getting together to pray. While parachurch organizations are sometimes instrumental in bringing gatherings like this about, I believe that churches, of their own volition, ought to be able to initiate such events and invite other churches to join with them. The success of this will of course depend to a large extent on how well the host church relates to the other churches in the area.

Evangelism

God did not commit the ministry of evangelism to any particular segment of the Christian church. The Lord did not commission only the Baptists or the Pentecostals (or any other group) to this ministry. Please remember that denominations as we know them in America did not exist in the days of the New Testament. The ministry of evangelism was committed to the whole church; texts that demonstrate this include Matthew 28:18–20; Acts 8:4; 11:19–20; and 1 Thessalonians 1:8. A quick survey of these texts hints at the fact that evangelism was done by both Jewish and Gentiles believers in Jesus, both men and women. This being the case, today all genuine believers in Jesus should participate in evangelism, and they should be able to join together and do it across denominational lines. This is another ministry in which parachurch organizations have helped mobilize churches. Organizations like the Billy Graham Evangelistic Association and Campus Crusade for Christ have served as facilitators of evangelism. While this is commendable, it seems that Bible-believing churches ought to be able, through their own initiative, to partner in evangelism for the purpose of reaching their own cities or towns. The basic gospel message should be a unifying force. Churches, and church leaders, need to lay down the "competition mindset" and develop a "kingdom mindset." We are called to build the kingdom of God, not our own churches. I believe that if we will honor that principle and labor with the kingdom of God in mind, God will take care of our individual churches.

Ministries of Mercy

Ministries of mercy such as feeding the poor, giving clothing to the needy, and caring for the sick are not practiced by some evangelicals; they see these things as social concerns, not spiritual matters. It is clear from Matthew 25 that Jesus placed a great deal of emphasis on them. If believers do not help those in need, they are not ministering to Jesus (see Matt 25:45). Commenting on this passage, Ron Sider has said that the Bible is very clear that those who could help the poor, but don't, go to hell.[2] Those are strong words but perhaps ones that we need to hear in order to wake us up. Care for the poor was part of Jewish piety (Exod 23:11; Lev 19:10; 23:22; Deut 15:7–8; Prov 29:7; 31:9). The New Testament also teaches the importance of care for the poor; ministries of mercy are to be done by the followers of Jesus. We have already seen that Matthew 25 teaches this truth. It is also taught in other places in the New Testament; is taught by both precept and example. A sampling of texts that show us that care for the poor is part of the Christian faith include Acts 9:36; 24:17, Romans 15:26; Galatians 2:10; and James 2:15–16. Ministries of mercy is an area in which cooperation in the body of Christ should not be a problem. After all, it is not a subject about which there should be much doctrinal dispute; the Bible is very clear about it—it is a matter of practical help. Partnering in this area could include having a joint clothing drive to help supply a shelter with clothing or having a number of local churches contribute to a food pantry that is housed in one local church. The church should be the first to model the graciousness and generosity of God. This is an area in which cooperation may be especially important. Food and clothing can be expensive. If a number of churches band to-

---

2. Sider, *Rich Christians*, 78.

gether and pool their resources, they will be able to supply more needs than if they operate independently.

SUMMARY

I hope that this chapter has piqued your interest in networking and helped in some small way to show you that there are different possibilities to get your church involved in helping to make a greater difference in the world. I also hope that you will notice that some of these possibilities do not require large amounts of money, a big staff, or a lot of work to get started. Some of them can flow quite easily by allowing the life of Christ that we have in us to be expressed in the relationships that we already have. May the Lord open your eyes to the unique possibilities that he has placed within your reach. Remember, your church is one small expression of the body of Christ (even if you have many people in your church), and you are part of something much larger.

12

Answering the Prayer of Jesus

BOTH SCRIPTURE AND CHURCH history testify to the difficulty of having, and maintaining, unity in the church. This is true both in regard to the local congregation and with reference to relationships between congregations within a community or area. However, I do not believe that the quest for unity is "mission impossible." I believe that biblical unity, not uniformity, is possible to have. I say this with confidence for a number of reasons. First, Jesus prayed for unity; it is his desire. Second, the fact that he prayed for unity also indicates that it is the will of God the Father. Jesus always prayed in his Father's will. This should give us great hope that our quest for unity is a very real possibility. Third, our confidence can further be bolstered by the fact that Jesus' prayers are always answered! And fourth, we can have confidence that unity is possible from some of the material in the preceding chapters. In earlier chapters I have shown that unity is possible; we have seen concrete examples of it. We have looked at various texts in the New Testament and seen that, at times, the early church was united. We have also seen there are signs of unity in the contemporary church. There is evidence of this both in the United States and overseas. In spite of these encouraging signs, there is no denying that the church still has a long way to go with regard to the issue of unity. In 1977 this prophetic word was given at the Charismatic Conference in Kansas City:

Mourn and weep,
for the body of my Son is broken.
Mourn and weep,
for the body of my Son is broken.
Come before me with broken hearts and contrite spirits,
for the body of my Son is broken.
Come before me with sackcloth and ashes,
Come before me with tears and mourning,
for the body of my Son is broken.

I would have made you one new man,
but the body of my Son is broken.
I would have made you a light on a mountaintop,
A city glorious and splendorous
that all the world would have seen,
but the body of my Son is broken.

The light is dim,
My people are scattered,
the body of my Son is broken.
I gave all I had
In the body and blood of my Son;
It spilled on the earth,
the body of my Son is broken.

Turn from the sins of your fathers
And walk in the ways of my Son.
Return to the plan of your Father,
Return to the purpose of your God;
the body of My Son is broken.
Mourning and weeping,
for the body of my Son is broken.[1]

This word is still in many ways relevant today. It is very important that unity be pursued because unity is God's stated purpose
for the church. This can be seen in Scripture and in this prophetic
word. The Spirit and the word agree. For unity to be restored to
the church we must pursue it; unity will not just happen if we

---

1. Manuel, *Like a Mighty River*, 195.

allow the status quo to remain. The effort exerted will be worth it. The benefits of unity have been stated before; the church will be able to accomplish more together than apart, and it will be a more convincing testimony to unbelievers that the Father sent the Son into the world. At the 1977 Charismatic Conference held in Kansas City this prophetic word was also given:

> I speak a word of repentance to my Church. I am not pleased with the state of my Church, the condition of my people. There is much separation, there is suspicion and hostility among you, there is fear and mistrust among you, there is argumentativeness among you. This should not be so, my people. I call on each and every one of you to repent, to turn away from the sin of unforgiveness, of hardness of heart. . . .[2]

So what can be done to help foster unity? The prophetic word said that the church needs to repent; that is, it needs to change. The church needs to conform to God's agenda. But what kinds of change are necessary? What specific things need to take place in order to move the church further down the road toward Christian unity? Let us turn our attention now to some practical things that can be done to help bring the body of Christ more in line with God's desire of unity for his people.

MOVING DOWN THE ROAD

I think that in order for the church to make progress toward unity it must first acknowledge the disunity that exists. After that has been squarely faced, then I believe that there are four things that need to take place in the body of Christ on a widespread basis. These four things are recognition of the truth of Scripture, prayer, the active cooperation and involvement of church leadership, and sensitivity to and cooperation with the Holy Spirit.

2. Ibid., 114.

THE TRUTH OF THE SCRIPTURES

All born-again believers need to be thoroughly convinced that unity is God's desire. The prayer of Jesus in John 17 should make that clear. This conviction is absolutely vital. Christians will come to this conclusion if they study the Scriptures. Believers may not find a lot of good models for unity in church history, but they will find some good models in Scripture. The Bible is God's revelation to us; it is our primary source; it is God's word clear and unvarnished. Texts which indicate the divine origin of the Bible include 2 Timothy 3:16–17; 2 Peter 1:20–21; Acts 4:25; and 1 Thessalonians 1:5; 2:13. In addition, evidences such as fulfilled prophecy and historical accuracy help support the biblical claim that the Bible is of divine origin.[3] Many denominations have a document that they call a statement of faith or articles of faith. This document outlines the basic beliefs of that particular church group. Usually somewhere in that document is a statement to the effect that the Bible is their only rule, or guide, for faith and practice. This is as it should be. Scripture is to hold a place of authority in our lives (2 Tim 3:16–17; 4:2–4); we are to live by it (Matt 4:4). One of the subjects that the Bible addresses quite frequently is the subject of relationships, both the relationship of the human race to God and the relationship of people to one another.

Confronting the "Isms"

Believers need to come to Scripture and allow the word to speak to them regarding Christian unity. We looked at a number of the things that divide Christians and churches in chapters 3 through 5. In addition there are also some "isms" that divide us; I am speaking here specifically of racism, sexism, and denominationalism. We must allow the Lord to speak to us regarding these issues as well. Allowing the Lord, through the Scriptures, to confront these things will not be easy. It will be difficult because of the blind spots that we have due to teachings or practices that we

3. McDowell, *Evidence*, 12–13.

have come to accept as correct or normal. It will also be difficult because we tend to have certain defense mechanisms in place that help us justify divisions along these lines. Most of us do not like to think that we have any issues with sexism or racism; they not only sound evil; they are evil. They are marks of prejudice and partiality and ". . . God does not show favoritism."(Rom 2:11); as followers of Jesus, we are not supposed to show favoritism either (see Jas 2:1–4). We are to be impartial like our Lord.

Racism

Gordon-Conwell's Center for Urban Ministerial Education (CUME) periodically offers a course called "Christianity and the Problem of Racism." I heard one report that students in that class have cried as they have come to the awareness that they have been prejudiced or racist. Now keep in mind the people taking this course are Christians, born-again believers who are either already in Christian ministry or are preparing for it. It is a shocking revelation for a Christian to come to an awareness that such a sin is present in his or her life. To their credit these students did not dismiss or excuse the sin but were able to recognize the truth as painful as it was. In his book, *The Next Evangelicalism: Freeing the Church From Western Cultural Captivity*, Soong–Chan Rah gives examples of how racism has infiltrated the church.[4] For example, the Church Growth Movement promoted racism by its teaching of the homogenous unit principle.[5] This principle teaches that churches grow fastest when they are racially homogenous.[6] The Emerging Church Movement tends toward racism because it is largely a white movement, and it does not listen to other (non-white) voices.[7] Though these movements may not have consciously or intentionally sought to foster racism, it is

4. Rah, *The Next Evangelicalism*, 64–87.
5. Ibid., 98.
6. Ibid.
7. Ibid., 109, 119.

there nonetheless. As the Lord calls attention to this injustice, we need to repent and take appropriate steps to address it.

SEXISM

Another "ism" that we find in the church is sexism. I briefly touched on this in chapter 4 when I mentioned that one of the things that divides believers is the subject of women in ministry. Sexism sounds so worldly and unholy that we can not imagine it being present in the church, yet it is significantly and subtly present. The term *sexism* is repulsive to us because it sounds like the demeaning or subjugation of women. Soong-Chan Rah makes only a passing reference to sexism in his book. He acknowledges that it exists in the church, but he does not address it at any length. He refers to "the white male captivity of the American Evangelical church."[8]

Leaving the race issue aside for a moment, we must acknowledge that in some sectors of the church women are assigned a sort of "second-class citizen status." That is, they are barred from holding certain positions of leadership in the church; specifically, they are barred from being pastors or being in ministries in which they might exercise authority over men. In fairness it must be admitted that those who hold this view do not do so based solely on human preference but on a particular interpretation of Scripture.

Those who restrict the place of women do so largely on the basis of what Paul wrote in 1 Timothy 2:11–12. In this text Paul did prohibit women from teaching and holding authority over men. This is the only biblical text that explicitly prohibits women from teaching, and it seems to be at odds with what Paul says elsewhere about the ministry of women.[9] New Testament scholar, Craig Keener, thinks that it would be surprising if at least half of the body of Christ could be excluded from teaching on the basis of one verse.[10] In order to understand why Paul wrote what he did,

8. Ibid., 22.
9. Keener, *Paul, Women & Wives*, 101.
10. Ibid.

one needs to understand some of what was happening in Ephesus at that time. Royce Gruenler's article *The Mission-Lifestyle Setting of 1 Tim 2:8-15* is one resource that will help clarify the situation that Paul was addressing in 1 Timothy.[11] Gilbert Bilezikian says that as we try to adopt a correct theology regarding women in ministry we should choose the option that will help God's work, not hinder it.[12] This is not to say that we should develop our belief and practice based on logic; we should develop our beliefs and practices based on the whole of what Scripture teaches.

A discussion of the subject of women in ministry is beyond the scope of this book. Many books have been written about this subject. For those who are concerned that placing women in positions of teaching and leadership would violate Scripture, I would suggest two books to you, Aída Besançon Spencer's *Beyond the Curse: Women Called to Ministry*[13] and Craig S. Keener's *Paul, Women & Wives: Marriage and Women's Ministry in the Letters of Paul.*[14] Both of these resources will prove very valuable in helping put the issue of women in ministry in proper biblical perspective. These books will also demonstrate that allowing women full rights in ministry is not a part of the liberal agenda but is in fact a matter of scriptural truth.

Denominationalism

Denominationalism is not usually looked upon as evil; it is generally seen in a more favorable light. Of the three "isms" that I have mentioned, this is probably the least offensive. Allegiance to a denomination is seen as a form of loyalty to a group and, of course, to God and his truth. We may at times attempt to justify denominationalism from the Bible, even though they did not have denominations in the church of the first-century. However, we do see one sign of "the party spirit" emerge even in the days

11. Gruenler, *The Mission-Lifestyle*, 215–18.

12. Bilezikian, *Community 101*, 82.

13. Spencer, *Beyond the Curse*.

14. Keener, *Paul, Women & Wives*.

of Jesus, a kind of prefiguring or foreshadowing of denomina-tionalism in the New Testament itself. In Mark 9:38, the disciples tell Jesus that they saw a man casting out demons in his name; because this person was not a part of "their group," they told the man to stop. In Mark 9:39 we find that Jesus told his disciples that they shouldn't have done that. Please note that Jesus expressed his disapproval of this.

Today we may attempt to justify our divisions and say that our various denominational separations show which of us have the Lord's approval and which do not (1 Cor 11:19). Of course the group that we are a part of has the Lord's approval! We might also contend that if people were really true believers they would have remained with us (1 John 2:19) and not broken off to form or be part of another group. Certainly there are circumstances in which these texts have relevance. This was true in the New Testament church, and it is true in the contemporary church as well. However, in most cases I would say that we probably cannot legitimately appeal to verses like these as justification for the lack of unity in the body of Christ. We do not always recognize some of the exclusionary aspects of denominationalism and how they work contrary to Jesus' prayer and desire. Don't get me wrong; I am *not* against denominations. Let me say it again: I am *not* against denominations; I am a part of one. God can and does use denominations for good. But the negativity of the "ism" is still with us, and we need to address it.

I dare say that almost all of the things that we believers do we justify as being "scriptural." If they were not, we would not do them, right? After all, as sons and daughters of God, we would not purposely seek to disobey him. Coming to terms with our blind spots and misunderstandings of Scripture and acknowl-edging that our particular group does not have the market on truth cornered will be a challenge. It will mean not only that we admit that we have been wrong in some ways, but also that we will have to set aside our previous assumptions and learn not only to think differently, but also to act differently. We will have to realign ourselves with the truth. In addition we will have to come to the place of realizing that not all truths are equally important, that there are things on which we need to allow some flexibility.

For example, as Bible-believing Christians we must believe that salvation is found in Christ alone (John 14:6; Acts 4:12; 1 Tim 2:5–6). This is a non-negotiable. However, those who believe that salvation is found only in Christ differ on some points. Some Christians hold to a Calvinistic view, which emphasizes God's choice in the matter, and some hold to an Arminian viewpoint which emphasizes humanity's exercise of free will with regard to salvation. Both of these views fall within the parameters of orthodoxy, and both can cite Scripture to support their particular view. We need to keep in mind that Calvinism and Arminianism are human constructs, based on biblical truth, that have been developed to try to explain important aspects of our salvation. I do not think that the church should be divided over the secondary aspects of the doctrine of salvation. I think that this should hold true for other doctrines as well.

Eschatology is another case in point. There are, among Bible-believing Christians, many divergent views regarding specific details of the end times. I think that all Bible-believing Christians would agree that we believe in the personal, visible return of Jesus Christ to the earth. This is the major truth that we should focus on, not the smaller details that tend to divide us.

PRAYER

Prayer is essential to the pursuit of Christian unity. The Scriptures give us ample proof of its importance. The most important illustration is the example of the Lord Jesus. Jesus prayed that his people would be one, that they would be united (John 17:21, 23). If he prayed for our unity, then it must be important. In addition to his example, we find the apostle Paul praying for the unity of the Roman church (Rom 15:5–6). So there is biblical warrant for praying for unity.

In more recent times the importance of prayer for Christian unity has also been recognized. In the days of the Charismatic Movement there was a song that was quite popular. This song mentioned the importance of prayer for the unity of Christ's church. The first verse of the song said,

> We are one in the Spirit,
> we are one in the Lord.
> We are one in the Spirit,
> we are one in the Lord.
> And we pray that all unity
> may one day be restored.[15]

This song astutely points out two realities. The first reality is that all genuine Christians have the Holy Spirit; the Spirit lives in all believers (Rom 8:9; Eph 1:13; Heb 6:4). This is true regardless of the denomination or church that one is part of. The Holy Spirit is the one who unifies us; this can be seen from a couple of other texts. In 1 Corinthians 12:13 we are told that the Holy Spirit baptizes all believers into the body of Christ. Ephesians 4:3 tells us that as believers we are to work to keep the unity that the Holy Spirit has already given us. The second reality is that even though God has united us by the Holy Spirit at a practical level, there is much division or brokenness in the body of Christ. Since this is true, we ought to pray, as the song says, for unity to be restored to Christ's body.

THE INVOLVEMENT OF CHURCH LEADERSHIP

The third thing that is necessary in order for the church to move down the road toward unity involves the active participation of church leadership. In the Bible we see the leaders of the New Testament church working for unity. These leaders labored long and hard to bring the people of God together around the Lord and scriptural truth. As they labored toward this end, we in the

15. Peter Scholtes, "They'll Know We Are Christians," 1966 F.E.L Publications, assigned 1991 to Lorenz Publishing Company. All rights reserved.

modern-day church, need to follow their example because the need for unity is still present. Church leaders need to actively and intentionally preach and teach on the subject of Christian unity. All believers are never going to agree on every fine point of doctrine. However, church leaders need to be able to differentiate between doctrines that are non-negotiable and those that we can extend some charity on and allow for some diversity of thought. Genuine believers agree on the essentials of the faith, and leaders ought to help their congregations see that and focus on that. Leaders need to "accentuate the positive." There should be no "irreconcilable differences" among Christian churches when it comes to cardinal doctrines of the faith. It is more helpful and beneficial to focus on the things that unite us than on the denominational distinctives that divide us.

Leaders need to show their congregations that unity is a scriptural truth, that it is the will of God, and that it reflects the heart and prayer of Jesus. They need to set this truth forth plainly. There are two reasons for this. First, the declaration of the word is a responsibility that is squarely laid at their feet; they are to preach and teach it (2 Tim 4:2; 1 Tim 4:13). One of the qualifications for elders is that they be able to teach (1 Tim 3:2; Titus 1:9). Church leaders are to declare the word of God because it is of benefit (2 Tim 3:16). Using Paul as a model, church leaders should declare the whole will of God (Acts 20:27). More specific to the purpose of this book, Paul tells us that one of the tasks of church leaders such as apostles, prophets, evangelists, pastors, and teachers is to bring God's people to unity in the faith (Eph 4:13). Paul was constantly trying to bring unity to the churches that he planted. He also sought to bring unity or mutual cooperation between churches in different locations, most notably between Jewish and Gentile churches.

Preaching and teaching are good starting points for leaders to move their congregations toward unity with the larger body of Christ, but unity requires more than words; it requires action. This is important because "as the leader goes, so go the people."

Congregations will do what they see their leaders do. Example is a powerful teacher; in fact, in some cases it may even more powerful than the spoken word. If the leadership of a given church is strongly denominational and sectarian, the congregation will probably be the same; they will follow their leader's teaching and example. If the leadership preaches unity but practices separation, the people are more likely to follow their example than their words. As the late Esther Rollins, one of my instructors at Zion Bible Institute used to say, "Your actions speak so loudly I can't hear what you say." The Scriptures are clear that the Lord wants the church to be united. Below is another prophetic word from the Charismatic Conference of 1977 which also stresses this truth and gives church leaders the responsibility to promote unity:

> The Lord has a word to speak to the leaders of the Christian Churches—to the leaders of *all* the Christian churches—and if you are a bishop, or a superintendent, or a supervisor, or an overseer, or the head of a Christian movement or organization, and that includes many of us here, this word is for you. Because the Lord says, you are all guilty in my eyes for the condition of my people, who are weak and divided and unprepared. I have set you in office over them, and you have not fulfilled that office, as I would have it fulfilled. Because you have not been the servants that I have called you to be. This is a hard word, but I want you to hear it.
>
> You have not come to me and made important in your lives and in your efforts those things which were most important to me, but instead you chose to put other things first. And you have tolerated division amongst yourselves and grown used to it, and you have not repented for it and fasted for it, or sought me to bring it to an end. But you have tolerated it and increased it. And you have not been my servants first of all in every case, but you have served other people ahead of me, and you have served the world ahead of me, and you have served your organizations ahead of me. But I am God, and you are my servants; why are you not serving me first of all?

> I know your hearts, and I know that many of you love
> me, and I have compassion on you, and I have placed
> you in a very high place. But I have placed you there,
> and I call you to account for it. Now, humble yourselves
> before me and come to me in repentance, in fasting,
> mourning, and weeping for the condition of my people.
> Because if you do not humble yourselves now and seek
> me earnestly, then my people will be unprepared for the
> difficulties that lie ahead.[16]

The active participation of church leadership is absolutely essential to moving the church down the road toward unity so that their congregations will see that they are in fact spiritually joined to all believers everywhere who call on the name of the Lord Jesus Christ (see 1 Cor 1:2).

SENSITIVITY TO THE HOLY SPIRIT

A fourth essential to moving the church down the road toward biblical unity is sensitivity to the Holy Spirit. We, like the churches in Revelation chapters 2 and 3, need to be able to hear what the Spirit is saying to the church (Rev 2:7, 11, 17, 29; 3:6, 13, 22). While all believers are not equally sensitive or open to the Holy Spirit, as the previously cited verses in Revelation indicate, sensitivity to the Spirit is a quality that can and should be developed. This is possible because all genuine believers are partakers of the Holy Spirit (Rom 8:9; Eph 1:13; Heb 6:4). The Spirit lives in each believer and is the one who places each believer in the body of Christ (1 Cor 12:13). All Christians hold the Spirit in common regardless of the Christian denomination that they are a part of. The Holy Spirit ministers to the life of the believer in a number of ways: the Spirit convicts, comforts, indwells, sanctifies, and empowers. All of these aspects of the Spirit's work can be directed toward the individual or the corporate body. The Spirit is present with us; we just need to discipline ourselves to be aware of his presence in and with us. As we do so, we need to

16. Manuel, 193.

be careful not to overlook another big part of what the Spirit is trying to do in the church at large. The Spirit is trying to unite God's people. Paul wrote about this in his letter to the church in Ephesus. In Ephesians 4:3 he said, "Make every effort to keep the unity of the Spirit through the bond of peace." This verse indicates that there is a unity that the Holy Spirit provides to the people of God, and it is our responsibility to cooperate with what the Spirit is trying to accomplish.

The Holy Spirit sometimes does things that are disturbing to the church. One example of this relates to the subject of unity. I touched on this example back in chapter 2. In Acts 10 the apostle Peter, who was a Jew, went to the home of a centurion named Cornelius. Cornelius was a Gentile. Peter went to this man's house after the Lord dealt with him through a vision of a sheet and the direct leading of the Holy Spirit. The result of all of this was that a number of Gentiles came to faith in Jesus. Peter's journey to the home of Cornelius did not win him any acclaim in the church in Jerusalem; in fact, they "called him on the carpet" because he had gone into the home of a Gentile and ate with Gentiles (Acts 11:3). In Acts 11 Peter set forth his case, relaying to the people in the Jerusalem church precisely what had happened (Acts 11:4). As he described in detail what took place, he specifically mentioned that the Spirit had directed him to go to Cornelius' house. He later mentioned that the Gentiles received the same gift, the Holy Spirit, in the same way as the Jewish believers had on the day of Pentecost in Acts 2. When Peter said that, the believers in Jerusalem stopped their criticism of Peter and praised God that the Lord had granted the Gentiles repentance to life (Acts 11:18). All turned out well here, but initially, because Peter followed the Holy Spirit, it got him in trouble with the church. The Lord was showing the church that there was to be unity between Jewish and Gentile believers; God had accepted them both.

In more recent times there was a man who got into trouble with his denomination for following the Holy Spirit. David Du Plessis, a Pentecostal minister who came to be know as "Mr. Pentecost," lost his credentials with the Assemblies of God for a period of time because he ministered in liberal circles like the National Council of Churches and the World Council of Churches.[17]

Below is another prophetic word given at the Charismatic Conference of 1977. This prophecy is another testimony of what the Lord wants to do in the church.

> Mark down this day and remember it,
> And write down this word and recall it,
> Because my promises will never fail,
> And no word that I speak falls to the ground,
> But I will fulfill it, every word.
> Remember it, call it to mind, declare it publicly;
> Have no fear, because I am faithful to my word,
> And I will fulfill it.
>
> I am going to restore my people and reunite them.
> I am going to restore to my people
> the glory that is mine.
> So that the world will not mock it or scorn it,
> But so that the world might know
> that I am God and King,
> And that I have come to redeem and save this earth.
>
> Yes, mark it down and remember
> That I have told you that I am restoring my people,
> Bestowing upon them power and glory,
> Bringing back to them the glory
> that is proper to my people,
> And making them look again like a kingdom,
> The Kingdom of God on this earth.[18]

Throughout this book I have cited various prophetic words that were given at the Charismatic Conference of 1977; perhaps this has made you uncomfortable. Maybe you do not share my conviction that the gift of prophecy still functions in the contemporary church. I have done this only to support things that the Scriptures already teach. The Spirit and the word agree. This

17. Du Plessis as told to Slosser, *A Man Called Mr. Pentecost*, 191–98.

18. Manuel, 79.

should not be surprising since the Spirit was actively involved in giving us the Scripture (2 Pet 1:20–21). While the 2 Peter reference is referring to the Old Testament Scriptures, this is true of the New Testament writings as well.

I believe that, just as in the days of the New Testament, the Holy Spirit is working today to bring greater unity to the body of Christ. The Spirit is at work breaking down barriers and prejudices that have long kept the people of God apart. Denominationalism is on the decline. The decline in denominationalism can be seen in two ways. First, as others have noted, many people no longer stay in the same denomination all of their lives. People seem to be much freer about venturing out to be part of a church that is different from the one they were raised in (if they had any Christian roots). Second, many churches are removing denominational labels from their names. Words like *Baptist,* and *Pentecostal,* are being dropped from church names and being replaced with words like *Community* and *International.* God is actively working to answer the prayer of Jesus.

DECISION TIME

In this book we have studied the subject of Christian unity. As we have done so, we have seen the obstacles to unity and the possibilities of actually having it. It is a challenge to be sure. Attaining and maintaining unity will not be easy, but the Scriptures indicate that it is not impossible. So now each of us is faced with a decision. Will we be part of the solution or part of the problem? Will we be a person who actively works to help bring about unity in the wider body of Christ or will we not? There is no neutral ground here. If we are not going to actively pursue unity through partnerships, we are casting a vote for things to remain the same. As the New Testament writers have shown us, unity is something that must be actively worked for. Are we as individuals prepared to invest our time and effort in pursuing unity? If you are a Christian leader, this question is especially important for you because you have the potential to influence and mobilize the people in your congregation toward unity. Will you actively involve yourself in the pursuit of unity? Will you preach the message of unity that is found in the Bible? Will you obey the prompting of the Holy Spirit who is working to bring the people of God together? Will you establish partnerships with other churches locally, nationally, or internationally? Will you reach out to link arms with believers in churches other than yours? In short, will you answer the prayer of Jesus in John 17? The speed with which the prayer of Jesus is answered in some measure depends on each of us. This is the moment of decision—what will you do? We know what Jesus wants; he prayed for it in John 17. He prayed that his people would be one (John 17:21). I hope that you will decide to be part of the answer to his prayer.

Bibliography

Barrett, C. K. *The Pastoral Epistles*. Grand Rapids, MI: Outreach Publications, 1986.

Bilezikian, Gilbert. *Community 101*. Grand Rapids, MI: Zondervan/Willowcreek Resources, 1997.

Brown, Michael L. *Answering Jewish Objections to Jesus*. Vols. 1-4. Grand Rapids, MI: Baker, 2000–2007. Vol. 5. San Francisco, CA: Purple Pomegranate Productions, 2010.

Bruce, F. F. *Commentary on the Book of Acts*. Grand Rapids, MI: Eerdmans, reprint, 1980.

CCCNE Web site. http://www.cccne.org/mission_mission.htm, viewed January, 2010.

Cook, Jerry, with Stanley C. Baldwin. *Love, Acceptance, and Forgiveness: Being Christian in a Non-Christian World*. Ventura, CA: Regal, 2009.

Cordeiro, Wayne. *Doing Church as a Team*. Ventura, CA: Regal, 2001.

Douglas, J. D., et al., eds. *New Bible Dictionary*. 2nd ed. Wheaton, IL: Tyndale, 1982.

Du Plessis, David, as told to Bob Slosser. *A Man Called Mr. Pentecost*. Plainfield, NJ: Logos International, 1977.

Elwell, Walter A., and Robert W. Yarbrough, eds. *Encountering the New Testament*. Grand Rapids, MI: Baker, 1998.

Erickson, Millard J. *Christian Theology*. 2nd edition. Grand Rapids, MI: Baker, 1998.

Fee, Gordon D. *1 & 2 Timothy, Titus, New International Biblical Commentary*. Peabody, MA: Hendrickson, 1988.

———. *Paul's Letter to the Philippians. The New International Commentary on the New Testament*. Grand Rapids, MI: Eerdmans, 1995.

———. *The First Epistle to the Corinthians. The New International Commentary on the New Testament*. Grand Rapids, MI: Eerdmans, 1987.

Fee, Gordon D., and Douglas Stuart. *How to Read the Bible for All It's Worth*. 2nd edition. Grand Rapids, MI: Zondervan, 1993.

Frangipane, Francis. *A House United: How Christ-Centered Unity Can End Church Division*. Grand Rapids, MI: Chosen, 2005.

Gillquist, Peter F. *Let's Quit Fighting About the Holy Spirit*. Grand Rapids. MI: Zondervan, 1974.

Grudem, Wayne A., gen. ed. *Are Miraculous Gifts For Today?: Four Views.* Grand Rapids, MI: Zondervan, 1996.

Gruenler, Royce Gordon. *The Mission-Lifestyle Setting of 1 Timothy 2:8–15* JETS 41/2 (1998) 215–18.

Guthrie, Donald. *New Testament Introduction*, revised edition. Downers Grove, IL: InterVarsity, 1990.

The Jesus Film, 25th Anniversary edition. Orlando, FL: Campus Crusade for Christ International, 2003.

Keener, Craig S. *Paul, Women and Wives: Marriage and Ministry in the Letters of Paul.* Peabody, MA: Hendrickson, 1992.

————. *The IVP Bible Background Commentary: New Testament.* Downers Grove, IL: InterVarsity Academic, 1993.

King, John. *Can You See God in This Picture?: A Letter to My Sons Making Sense of 25 Years as a Pastor.* Waltham, MA: J. Timothy King, 2008.

Manuel, David. *Like a Mighty River.* Orleans, MA: Rock Harbor Press, 1977.

McDowell, Josh. *The New Evidence That Demands a Verdict.* Nashville, TN: Thomas Nelson, 1999.

Mead, Frank S. *Handbook of Denominations in the United States.* 6th ed. Nashville, TN: Abingdon, 1975.

Oss, Douglas A. "A Pentecostal/Charismatic View," *Are Miraculous Gift For Today?: Four Views.* Grand Rapids, MI: Zondervan, 1996.

Otis Jr., George, dir. *An Unconventional War*, Global Net Productions, The Sentinel Group, 2006.

Pentecost, J. Dwight. *Things to Come: A Study in Biblical Eschatology.* Grand Rapids, MI: Zondervan, 1964.

Pierce, Ronald W., and Rebecca Merrill Groothuis. gen. eds. *Discovering Biblical Equality: Complementarity Without Hierarchy.* Grand Rapids, MI: InterVarsity, 2004.

Rah, Soong–Chan. *The Next Evangelicalism: Freeing the Church from Western Cultural Captivity.* Downers Grove, IL: InterVarsity, 2009.

Scholtes, Peter. "They'll Know We Are Christians." 1966. F.E.L Publications, assigned 1991 to Lorenz Publishing Company. All rights reserved.

Sider, Ronald J., John M. Perkins, et al. *Linking Arms, Linking Lives.* Grand Rapids, MI: Baker, 2008.

Sider, Ronald J. *Rich Christians in an Age of Hunger: Moving From Affluence to Generosity.* 20th Anniversary edition. Dallas, TX: Word, 1997.

Snodgrass, Klyne. *The NIV Application Commentary: Ephesians.* Grand Rapids, MI: Zondervan, 1996.

Spencer, Aída Besançon. *Beyond the Curse: Women Called to Ministry.* Peabody, MA: Hendrickson, 1989.

Stedman, Ray C. *Authentic Christianity.* Waco, TX: Word, 1975.

————. *Body Life.* Ventura, CA: Regal, 1972.

Stott, John. *The Gospel & the End of Time: The Message of 1 & 2 Thessalonians.* Downers Grove, IL: InterVarsity, 1991.

————. *The Spirit, the Church and the World*. Downers Grove, IL: InterVarsity, 1990.

————. Plenary session of the Evangelistic Association of New England's Congress, 1995.

Wagner, C. Peter. *Your Spiritual Gifts Can Help Your Church Grow*. Ventura, CA: Regal, 1994.

Walvoord, John F., and Roy B. Zuck, eds. *The Bible Knowledge Commentary: New Testament*. Wheaton, IL: Victor, 1983.

Wiersbe, Warren. *The Bible Exposition Commentary: New Testament Vol. 2*. Colorado Springs, CO: Victor/Cook Communications Ministries, 2001.

Wilson, Marvin R. *Our Father Abraham: Jewish Roots of the Christian Faith*. Grand Rapids, MI: Eerdmans, 1989.

Witherington, Ben. *Conflict & Community in Corinth: A Socio-Rhetorical Commentary on 1 and 2 Corinthians*. Grand Rapids, MI: Eerdmans, 1995.